Contents Guide

Welcome & What You'll Learn

Welcome to the exciting world of ServiceNow ITSM! This book is your comprehensive guide to transforming IT service delivery within your organization using ServiceNow's powerful platform. If you're an ITSM professional, a system administrator, a ServiceNow developer, or simply curious about how to elevate your IT service processes, this book offers valuable insights and practical guidance.

Why ServiceNow ITSM?

Today's organizations grapple with the challenge of managing a sprawling IT environment that supports ever-evolving business needs. Inefficient processes, siloed information, and a lack of visibility lead to delayed responses, frustrated users, and mounting operational costs. ServiceNow ITSM offers a unified platform to streamline and automate crucial IT service processes, fostering greater efficiency, collaboration, and ultimately, enhanced customer satisfaction.

What You Will Master

This book takes a deep dive into the core ITSM processes supported by ServiceNow. You'll learn how to harness these industry-aligned modules to transform your IT operations:

- **Incident Management:** Swiftly respond to unplanned service disruptions, minimize downtime, and restore critical functions by leveraging ServiceNow's robust incident management capabilities.
- **Problem Management:** Proactively identify root causes of recurring incidents, implement long-term resolutions, and prevent future outages with ServiceNow's problem management features.
- **Request Fulfillment:** Efficiently handle and fulfill standard IT service requests, ensuring a seamless user experience.
- **Change Management:** Plan, approve, and execute changes to your IT infrastructure in a controlled, streamlined, and risk-averse manner.
- **Configuration Management Database (CMDB):** Establish a centralized repository of IT assets (Configuration Items) and their relationships, enabling informed decision-making, change impact analysis, and efficient troubleshooting.
- **Knowledge Management:** Create a robust knowledge base for common issues and solutions. Empower your users with self-service capabilities while reducing the burden on support teams.
- **Service Level Management:** Maintain service quality by setting clear expectations, defining Service Level Agreements (SLAs), and tracking performance metrics.

The Learning Journey

Here's a breakdown of what you can expect this book to cover:

Section 1: Foundation of ITSM

- **Unveiling IT Service Management (ITSM):** Gain a solid understanding of the fundamental concepts, principles, and frameworks that underpin ITSM best practices.
- **Understanding the Framework of ITSM:** Explore ITIL (and other relevant ITSM frameworks) that provide a structured approach to managing IT services.
- **Exploring ServiceNow Essentials (Part One & Two):** Become familiar with ServiceNow's intuitive interface, core functionalities, navigation, and essential administration tools.

Section 2: Mastering ITSM Processes

- **Navigating Incident Management to Optimize Request Management:** Learn the ins and outs of incident creation, categorization, prioritization, resolution, and closure within ServiceNow. Master the tools and techniques for effective request management to streamline user workflows.
- **Demystifying Problem Management to Enhancing Change Management:** Develop a deep understanding of Proactive and Reactive problem management approaches with practical insights. Dive into ServiceNow's change management process, exploring different change models and how to ensure smooth implementation.
- **Unveiling the Power of CMDB to Mastering Service Level Management:** Learn best practices for establishing a robust CMDB, maximizing its value, and leveraging it for various ITSM processes. Master the core principles of Service Level Management and how to establish and monitor meaningful SLAs.

Conclusion

- A recap of the key takeaways and a look at the exciting possibilities ServiceNow offers to propel your IT service delivery into the future.

Additional Resources

To supplement your knowledge and stay updated on the evolving ServiceNow landscape, consider these resources:

- **ServiceNow Documentation:** https://docs.servicenow.com/
- **ServiceNow Community:** https://community.servicenow.com/

- **ServiceNow Training Courses**
  https://www.servicenow.com/services/training-and-certification.html
- **ITIL Foundation**
  https://www.axelos.com/certifications/itil-certifications/itil-foundation-certification

Let's Begin!

Get ready to embark on a transformative journey to master ServiceNow ITSM. By the end of this book, you'll be equipped to optimize IT processes, improve service quality, and drive customer satisfaction within your organization.

Let's get started!

Section 1:
Foundation of ITSM

Unveiling IT Service Management (ITSM)

In today's digitally driven world, businesses rely heavily on their IT infrastructure to deliver products, services, and exceptional customer experiences. Outages, slowdowns, and inefficiencies in IT operations can have significant repercussions, impacting productivity, revenue, and customer satisfaction. This is where IT Service Management (ITSM) enters the picture as a strategic discipline – it enables organizations to manage their IT services effectively, optimizing performance and aligning IT with business goals.

What is ITSM?

ITSM encompasses the processes, methodologies, and best practices employed by organizations to design, deliver, manage, and continuously improve their IT services. Unlike traditional IT support that focuses on a break-fix model, ITSM adopts a holistic approach, emphasizing:

- **Service-Centric Mindset:** ITSM shifts the focus from individual technologies to the value-driven IT services that support critical business functions.
- **Customer Focus:** Users become customers. ITSM aims to provide a user-centric approach, prioritizing customer needs, and ensuring their satisfaction.
- **Process-Driven Framework:** ITSM relies on structured processes to manage IT services, ensuring consistency, efficiency, and measurable outcomes.
- **Life Cycle View:** ITSM considers the entire IT service lifecycle, encompassing stages like strategy, design, transition, operation, and continuous improvement.
- **Governance and Metrics:** ITSM emphasizes governance, accountability, and the use of relevant metrics to measure performance and identify areas for improvement.

Key Goals of ITSM

- **Aligning IT with Business:** ITSM bridges the gap between technical and business goals. This ensures IT initiatives directly support broader organizational objectives.
- **Improved Service Quality:** ITSM focuses on delivering reliable, consistent, and high-quality IT services that meet the needs of the users and stakeholders.
- **Increased Operational Efficiency:** Streamlined processes, automation, and a focus on continuous improvement contribute to greater efficiency in IT operations.
- **Cost Optimization:** ITSM enables the identification of cost-effective service delivery methods and helps optimize IT budgets.
- **Enhanced Agility:** ITSM facilitates faster responses to changing business requirements and the adoption of new technologies.
- **Risk Mitigation:** A structured, process-oriented approach aids in managing and reducing IT-related risks to business continuity.

Core Components of ITSM

The IT Service Management domain encompasses a wide range of ITSM processes responsible for managing different aspects of service delivery. Some core components include:

- **Incident Management:** Restoring normal services as quickly as possible after an unplanned disruption.
- **Problem Management:** Identifying root causes of recurring incidents to prevent them and minimize their impact.
- **Change Management:** Implementing IT changes in a controlled, risk-managed manner.
- **Request Fulfillment:** Handling standard service requests from users efficiently.
- **Service Level Management:** Defining service targets, monitoring performance, and ensuring agreed-upon service quality.
- **Knowledge Management:** Creating and maintaining a knowledge base to empower users and support staff.
- **Configuration Management Database (CMDB):** Building a centralized repository of IT infrastructure components, their attributes, and relationships.

ITSM Frameworks & Best Practices

ITSM best practices are often codified in frameworks that provide guidance for organizations to implement and enhance ITSM processes. The most prominent ITSM framework is:

- **ITIL® (Information Technology Infrastructure Library):** A set of globally recognized best practices for ITSM. It offers a comprehensive approach to service management, covering various processes across the service lifecycle. ITIL continues to evolve, with the latest iteration being ITIL 4.

Other ITSM frameworks and standards include:

- **COBIT® (Control Objectives for Information and Related Technologies):** Provides governance and management models for IT, aligning IT with business goals.
- **ISO/IEC 20000:** An international standard for IT Service Management, setting out requirements for service providers to establish an effective ITSM system.

Benefits of Implementing ITSM

Adopting ITSM principles and practices yields numerous advantages for organizations, including:

- **Improved customer satisfaction**
- **Enhanced service reliability and availability**
- **Increased IT operational efficiency**
- **Reduced IT costs**
- **Optimized IT-driven business innovation**
- **Better risk management and compliance**

Let's move forward! In the next chapter, we'll delve deeper into the framework of ITSM, exploring ITIL and other relevant best practice models.

Additional Resources

- **COBIT®** https://www.isaca.org/resources/cobit
- **ISO/IEC 20000** https://www.iso.org/standard/71507.html

Understanding the Framework of ITSM

In the previous chapter, we unveiled IT Service Management (ITSM), highlighting its goals and benefits. In this chapter, we'll dive deeper to understand the backbone of ITSM – the frameworks and standards that provide organizations with a blueprint to structure and implement effective service management processes.

What is an ITSM Framework?

An ITSM framework offers a collection of best practices, processes, and guidelines that help organizations deliver and manage IT services. These frameworks are not rigid prescriptive models. Instead, they provide flexible guidance, allowing tailoring to suit an organization's specific needs, culture, structure, and scale.

Key Benefits of ITSM Frameworks

- **Common Language & Terminology:** Frameworks foster consistent understanding, communication, and collaboration across IT teams.
- **Proven Best Practices:** They incorporate real-world experiences and knowledge, saving organizations time and resources when implementing ITSM processes.
- **Reduced Complexity:** Frameworks break down large ITSM domains into manageable processes and activities.
- **Continuous Improvement:** A structured framework enables ongoing assessment and optimization of IT service management practices.

ITIL: The Foundation of ITSM Frameworks

The Information Technology Infrastructure Library (ITIL) is the most widely adopted and acclaimed ITSM framework globally. Let's delve into the core concepts of ITIL:

- **Service-Centric Focus:** ITIL champions a shift away from isolated technologies towards a holistic focus on delivering valuable IT services that align with business needs.
- **IT Service Lifecycle:** Originally, ITIL divided ITSM processes into a structured lifecycle model, including:
  - **Service Strategy:** Defining IT services, understanding business needs, and planning for service delivery.

- - **Service Design:** Designing IT services based on requirements, ensuring performance, availability, security, and cost-effectiveness.
  - **Service Transition:** Smoothly transitioning new or changed services into the operational environment.
  - **Service Operation:** Day-to-day management and support of live IT services.
  - **Continual Service Improvement (CSI):** Identifying and implementing opportunities to enhance service quality, efficiency, and effectiveness.
- **ITIL 4: The Latest Evolution** ITIL has undergone several revisions, and the latest iteration, ITIL 4, has introduced significant changes:
  - **Service Value System (SVS):** A flexible model encapsulating all elements needed to create value through IT services.
  - **Four Dimensions Model:** Ensures that services are designed and managed holistically, considering Organizations & People, Information & Technology, Partners & Suppliers, and Value Streams & Processes.
  - **Guiding Principles:** A set of key principles to guide service management decisions and actions.

Other Relevant ITSM Frameworks and Standards

While ITIL remains a dominant force, valuable insights can be drawn from other frameworks and standards:

- **COBIT® (Control Objectives for Information and Related Technologies):** A framework from ISACA, focusing on governance, risk management, compliance, and aligning IT initiatives with broader enterprise goals.
- **ISO/IEC 20000: IT Service Management Systems:** An international standard that defines specific requirements for organizations to establish an effective service management system.
- **FitSM:** A lightweight ITSM standard, particularly suitable for smaller organizations or those new to ITSM.
- **VeriSM™:** Focuses on incorporating emerging management practices like Agile, Lean, and DevOps to adapt IT service management to the new digital age.

Choosing the Right Framework

No single framework is inherently "best." The choice depends on your organization's unique circumstances:

- **Organizational Culture:** Consider how well a framework aligns with your organization's decision-making processes, management style, and adaptability.
- **Size and Complexity:** Smaller organizations might benefit from the simplicity of FitSM, while larger enterprises with diverse needs might prefer the comprehensiveness of ITIL.
- **Industry-Specific Standards:** Organizations in particular industries may need to comply with sector-specific standards or regulations that align closely with certain frameworks.
- **Integration with Existing Processes:** If your organization already uses Agile or DevOps, VeriSM may offer a more natural integration point.

Remember: Frameworks are guides and should not be blindly followed. Your organization always has the flexibility to adapt and tailor them as needed.

Conclusion

ITSM frameworks provide structured, best practice guidance for designing, delivering, and improving IT services. Understanding core frameworks like ITIL, as well as their complementary alternatives, equips you with essential knowledge for a successful ITSM journey.

Join me in the next chapter where we'll start exploring the ServiceNow platform and its fundamental concepts!

Additional Resources

- **COBIT® - ISACA:** https://www.isaca.org/resources/cobit
- **ISO/IEC 20000** https://www.iso.org/standard/71507.html
- **FitSM** https://fitsm.eu/
- **VeriSM™** https://verism.global/

Exploring ServiceNow Essentials: Part One

In the previous chapters, we laid the foundation, exploring ITSM concepts and frameworks. Now, it's time to introduce the powerful platform that helps bring these principles to life: ServiceNow. In this and the following chapter, we'll delve into ServiceNow and its essential features to set you up for successful ITSM practice.

What is ServiceNow?

ServiceNow is a cloud-based software-as-a-service (SaaS) platform. It provides a suite of applications designed to automate and streamline IT service management processes, supporting ITIL and other best practice models. ServiceNow has evolved to offer solutions beyond traditional IT, including customer service, HR service delivery, security operations, and more.

Key Features of ServiceNow

- **Intuitive User Interface:** ServiceNow offers a modern, user-friendly interface, promoting easy navigation and adoption.
- **Workflow Automation:** A core strength lies in its workflow engine, enabling the design and automation of complex processes, reducing manual effort and improving efficiency.
- **Customizable Forms & Tables:** Tables form the backbone of data in ServiceNow, and forms provide user interfaces. Both elements are highly customizable, allowing organizations to tailor data structure and interfaces.
- **Powerful Reporting and Analytics:** ServiceNow offers real-time dashboards and customizable reports for valuable insights into service performance.
- **Knowledge Management:** Built-in capabilities enable creation and management of a knowledge base to support users and service desk staff.
- **Integration Capabilities:** ServiceNow easily integrates with a vast range of third-party systems and tools.
- **Scalability and Accessibility:** As a cloud-based SaaS platform, ServiceNow scales readily to meet organization needs and can be accessed from anywhere with an internet connection.

The ServiceNow Architecture

Let's take a brief look under the hood:

- **Multi-Instance Architecture:** ServiceNow uses a multi-instance model, where each customer has a dedicated instance, ensuring data isolation.
- **Now Platform®:** The Now Platform serves as the core, offering the database, workflow engine, reporting capabilities, and fundamental services used by ServiceNow applications.
- **ITSM Applications:** Incident, Problem, Change Management, and other core ITSM modules are pre-built applications on the Now Platform.
- **Development Tools:** ServiceNow allows developers and administrators to create new applications, customize existing features, and build integrations.

Navigating the ServiceNow User Interface

Let's familiarize ourselves with the key elements of the ServiceNow interface:

- **Application Navigator:** The left-hand navigation menu provides access to different applications and modules within your instance. Typing in the filter navigator helps quickly find features.
- **Banner Frame:** This top frame displays your user information, settings, and a global search bar.
- **Content Frame:** The central area where lists of records, forms, dashboards, and other content are displayed.
- **Lists and Forms:**
  - **Lists:** Display multiple records from a table in a structured format, allowing sorting, filtering, and manipulation of the data.
  - **Forms:** Detailed views of a single record in a table. Used to view, create, or edit records.

Important Concepts

Let's introduce a few concepts you'll encounter throughout your ServiceNow journey:

- **Tables:** Fundamental data structures in ServiceNow. They store records of different types (e.g., incidents, problems, changes, users).
- **Records:** Individual entries within a table (e.g., a specific incident record). Each record has a unique number.

- **Fields:** Elements within a record that hold specific data (e.g., 'Short description', 'Priority', 'Assigned to').
- **Roles:** Roles determine what actions users can perform in ServiceNow. Common roles include 'admin' (extensive permissions) and 'itil' (ITSM-specific roles).

Common ServiceNow System Administrator Tasks

While your book primarily focuses on ITSM processes, awareness of basic system administration aids understanding:

- **Creating users and groups**
- **Managing roles and access control**
- **Customizing forms and fields**
- **Building simple reports**
- **Implementing basic workflows**

Getting Started & Access

Typically, users engage with ServiceNow through either a Self-Service Portal or a dedicated workspace designed for fulfilling specific roles. Individual users will need a ServiceNow account to access their assigned interface.

Let's Continue Exploring

In the next chapter (Part Two), we'll delve deeper into ServiceNow navigation, essential tools, and techniques for searching and finding information. Get ready to continue your journey!

Additional Resources

- **ServiceNow Documentation:** https://docs.servicenow.com/
- **ServiceNow Community:** https://community.servicenow.com/
- **ServiceNow Developer Site:** https://developer.servicenow.com/

Exploring ServiceNow Essentials: Part Two

In the previous chapter, we introduced ServiceNow and navigated the basics of its user interface. Now, let's go a step further and explore additional tools for effective use of the platform, making your ServiceNow experience smooth and productive.

Mastering the Application Navigator

The Application Navigator serves as your primary guide within ServiceNow. Let's understand how to leverage it effectively:

- **Favorites:** Frequently used applications and modules can be marked as 'Favorites' for quick access at the top of the navigator.
- **History:** ServiceNow keeps track of your recently visited modules and records, accessible under the 'History' tab – handy for jumping back to previous tasks.
- **Type-Ahead Search:** As you begin typing in the filter field, ServiceNow suggests matching applications, modules, and even specific records. This offers a fast and efficient way to navigate.
- **'All Applications':** Clicking the 'All Applications' tab expands the navigator to display the entire list of applications available within your ServiceNow instance.

Working with Lists and Forms

Lists and forms are the primary means of viewing and interacting with data within ServiceNow. Mastering these is essential.

- **Lists:**
  - **Column Sorting:** Clicking a column header allows you to sort the list in ascending or descending order.
  - **Filtering:** Use the filter row to build simple or complex queries. Examples:
    - 'Priority is Critical'
    - 'State is New'
    - 'Assignment group IS EMPTY'
  - **Context Menus:** Right-clicking on a record in a list brings up a context menu with relevant actions (e.g., Open, Assign to Me, Create Task).

- ○ **Grouping:** Records can be grouped by a specific field for better organization (e.g., Group by 'Category' to see incident counts or assignments).
- **Forms:**
  - ○ **Dot-walking:** Reference fields (fields that link to records in other tables) allow you to 'dot-walk' to related information. For example, on an incident form, you might see 'Caller.Department' to view the user's Department record.
  - ○ **Form Layouts:** Multiple form views might be available, tailored for different purposes. Switch views as needed (e.g., a simplified view for mobile devices).
  - ○ **UI Actions:** Buttons on a form trigger actions (e.g., Resolve Incident, Update, Save). Some are context-sensitive, appearing based on conditions.
  - ○ **Related Lists:** At the bottom of forms, you'll find related lists, displaying linked records from other tables (e.g., on an incident form, you might see a list of related problems or changes).

Searching for Information

ServiceNow offers multiple ways to find what you need:

- **Global Search:** The search bar at the top right searches across various parts of your instance, including records, knowledge articles, catalog items, etc.
- **Table-specific Search:** Within a List, a dedicated search field allows you to find records within that specific table.
- **Knowledge Base Search:** ServiceNow offers a separate search tool dedicated to knowledge articles.

Configuring Your User Experience

ServiceNow allows you to personalize your workspace in several ways:

- **Theme & Accessibility:** Under User Settings, explore theme options (light/dark modes) and accessibility features.
- **Form Layouts:** If you have the appropriate permissions, you can personalize form layouts by adding, removing, or rearranging fields.
- **List Column Options:** Select which columns appear in lists and their order.
- **Notifications:** Configure email or in-platform notifications for updates, assignments, and other events relevant to you.

Exploring Additional Useful Features

- **Reports:** ServiceNow comes with pre-built reports, and you can create your own custom reports to extract specific data.
- **Dashboards:** Present multiple reports and visualizations on a single screen for real-time monitoring of KPIs and service health.
- **Service Catalog:** A user-friendly interface for requesting services or items through pre-defined catalog categories.
- **Knowledge Base:** Create, publish, and search structured knowledge articles for self-help and troubleshooting by both users and support staff.

Conclusion

This chapter has equipped you with essential tools to confidently navigate ServiceNow. Remember, ongoing practice and exploration are key. Don't hesitate to experiment and leverage the abundant resources available to unlock the full power of the platform.

Additional Resources

- **ServiceNow Documentation - Searching**
  https://docs.servicenow.com/bundle/quebec-platform-user-interface/page/use/navigation/searching.html
- **ServiceNow Documentation - Working with Lists**
  https://docs.servicenow.com/bundle/quebec-platform-user-interface/page/use/navigation/list-concept.html
- **ServiceNow Documentation - Personalizing the interface**
  https://docs.servicenow.com/bundle/paris-platform-administration/page/administer/personalization/concept/c_Personalization.html

Section 2:
Mastering ITSM Processes

Navigating Incident Management: Insights and Strategies

Incident management is the cornerstone of IT service management. Its primary focus lies in restoring normal service operations as quickly as possible after unplanned disruptions, minimizing the impact on business operations and users. In this chapter, we'll delve into the strategies and processes employed within ServiceNow to manage incidents effectively, covering crucial processes such as logging, categorization, prioritization, resolution, and closure.

What is an Incident?

- An incident is an unplanned disruption or a degradation of the quality of an IT service.
- Incidents can also result from the failure of a configuration item (hardware, software, etc.) that has not yet impacted service.
- Examples of incidents include server outages, network issues, application errors, access problems, or even a broken printer.

The Incident Management Process

ServiceNow's Incident Management module adheres to industry best practices, providing a structured flow:

1. **Incident Logging:** The process begins with the creation of a new incident record. Incident logging can happen through various channels:
   - **Self-Service Portal:** Users log incidents directly via a user-friendly web interface.
   - **Email:** Incidents can be automatically created from designated email addresses.
   - **Phone Call:** Service desk agents can log incidents over the phone, then enter them into ServiceNow.

- **Alerts & Event Monitoring:** Integrated monitoring tools can automatically create incidents based on detected system events.
2. **Categorization & Prioritization:**
   - **Categorization:** Incidents are assigned to categories and sub-categories (e.g., Network > Connectivity, Software > Application Error) to aid in routing and reporting.
   - **Prioritization:** Incidents are assigned a priority based on their impact (How many users or services are affected?) and urgency (How quickly does it need to be resolved?). Common prioritization schemes include 'Critical,' 'High,' 'Medium,' and 'Low'.
3. **Initial Diagnosis:** The service desk or assigned support team conducts a preliminary investigation for:
   - **Reproducing the Issue:** Understanding the exact steps that led to the problem.
   - **Basic Troubleshooting:** Applying quick fixes or known workarounds.
   - **Information Gathering:** Collecting logs, configuration details, or additional user input.
4. **Investigation and Escalation:** If a simple solution isn't readily available, incidents might need deeper troubleshooting:
   - **Assignment:** The incident is assigned to the appropriate support group or individual with the necessary expertise.
   - **Escalation:** If needed, incidents can be escalated to higher tiers of support, more specialized teams, or external vendors, following predefined escalation processes.
5. **Resolution and Recovery:** Once the root cause is identified, technical teams implement a fix or change. Thorough testing ensures the service is restored.
6. **Closure:** After confirmation from the user, the incident is closed with the following:
   - **Resolution Details:** A clear description of the steps taken is documented.
   - **Knowledge Creation:** Relevant insights are captured to create knowledge base articles (KBA) for future reference.

Incident Management Best Practices

- **Communication is Key:** Keep users updated proactively on incident status, estimated resolution times, and workarounds. Clear communication minimizes frustration and builds trust.

- **Knowledge-Centered Support (KCS):** Encourage technicians to share solutions as knowledge base articles to enable self-service and reduce incident volume.
- **Problem Management Integration:** Regularly analyze incident data to identify recurring problems that warrant proactive problem investigation. Proactive Problem resolution prevents future incidents.
- **Incident Reporting & Analytics:** Track metrics like time to resolution, first-time fix rate, and incident volume to pinpoint bottlenecks and improvement opportunities.
- **Continual Improvement:** Continuously evaluate processes, communication, and self-service capabilities with the aim of optimization and efficiency.

ServiceNow Incident Management Tools

ServiceNow provides a robust toolkit to streamline incident handling:

- **Assignment Rules:** Automate incident routing based on criteria like category, location, or support group skills.
- **Work Notes vs. Additional Comments:** Utilize the distinction for internal versus user-visible communications.
- **Major Incident Management:** Dedicated processes for managing high-severity incidents that necessitate a coordinated, prioritized response.
- **Integration with Other Modules:** Seamlessly link incidents to problems, changes, or CMDB assets.

Conclusion

Effective incident management is the bedrock of reliable IT service delivery. By understanding the core processes, leveraging ServiceNow's tools, and adhering to best practices, you'll restore normalcy swiftly, reduce user downtime, and foster confidence in your IT operations.

In the next chapter, we'll discuss advanced strategies for handling major incidents and ensuring your IT organization is prepared for the critical moments.

Additional Resources

- **ServiceNow Documentation - Incident Management**
  https://docs.servicenow.com/bundle/quebec-it-service-management/page/product/incident-management/concept/c_IncidentManagement.html

Strategies for Effective Incident and Major Incident Management

In this chao, we'll discuss refined techniques for streamlining incident resolution, minimizing downtime, and establishing a robust major incident response plan for those critical, high-impact scenarios.

Incident Management Best Practices and Refinements

Let's enhance your incident management process with these valuable practices:

- **Prioritize, Prioritize!** A clear prioritization matrix (impact vs. urgency) helps the service desk focus on the most critical incidents affecting users and services.
- **Optimize Incident Routing and Assignment:** Automate as much as possible, utilizing service offerings, skills mapping, and availability for intelligent assignment to individuals or groups capable of swift resolution.
- **Communication During Outages:** Proactive communication through multiple channels (announcements in service portals, email, SMS) reduces inbound calls and improves the user experience during disruptions.
- **Swarming for Swift Resolution:** Enable collaborative problem-solving by bringing together technicians with diverse specializations and encouraging knowledge sharing via dedicated communication channels.
- **Post-Incident Review (PIR):** Schedule brief reviews after major incidents or those with potential for recurrence. Focus on identifying improvement opportunities and documenting key lessons learned.
- **Automation for Routine Tasks:** Leverage workflow automation tools and integrations to implement self-service password resets, automate access requests, and streamline other common low-complexity incidents.

The Role of Major Incident Management

Major incidents are those characterized by high severity, extensive impact, and critical urgency, often necessitating a much larger, coordinated response compared to standard incidents. ServiceNow has dedicated features for dealing with such critical situations.

Here's where major incident management steps in:

- **Rapid Mobilization of Resources:** Triggers specific communication processes, potentially notifying executives, external vendors, and key stakeholders.
- **Dedicated Workspace:** ServiceNow provides a centralized workspace for managing major incidents, enhancing collaboration and visibility for everyone involved.
- **Structured Communication:** Predefined communication plans ensure updates are provided, and a clear command structure is followed to avoid confusion.
- **Post-Incident Analysis:** Major incidents demand a thorough root cause analysis and review to learn preventive measures, and improve response plans.

Key Considerations for Major Incident Management

1. **Define Clear Triggers:** Determine the criteria for designating an incident as 'major' (e.g., complete outage of a critical service, significant financial or reputational risk).
2. **Dedicated Communications Plan:** Develop pre-written templates, contact lists, and update intervals to keep everyone informed during a crisis.
3. **Major Incident Roles:** Pre-assign roles like communication lead, technical lead, and overall incident commander to establish a response structure.
4. **Practice Makes Perfect:** Regularly run simulated major incident drills to test your processes, communication, and team readiness.

Incident Management Tools for Enhanced Effectiveness

Explore these powerful features in ServiceNow to further optimize your incident handling:

- **On-call Management:** Automate the scheduling, escalations, and notifications related to out-of-hours support using ServiceNow's on-call functionalities.
- **Visual Task Boards (VTB):** Break down complex incidents into smaller tasks and track their progress in real-time. VTBs are ideal for collaborative resolution or major incident handling.

- **Mobile Capabilities:** Empower technicians with access to essential ServiceNow incident information and tools on their smartphones for greater flexibility.
- **Walk-up Experience:** Enable users to log and receive in-person support at designated walk-up locations (particularly helpful in service desk scenarios).
- **Vendor Management Integration:** Manage communications with external suppliers and track their SLAs within ServiceNow, especially vital during incidents involving third-party components.

Metrics for Success

To assess your incident management efficiency, track these key metrics:

- **Mean Time to Resolve (MTTR):** Average time it takes to resolve incidents.
- **First Time Fix Rate:** Percentage of incidents resolved on the first assignment, indicating efficient problem diagnosis and knowledge availability.
- **Incidents by Priority:** Helps track the severity of incidents and resource allocation.
- **User Satisfaction:** Gauge user satisfaction with incident resolution through surveys and feedback.

Conclusion

By implementing these strategies and making the most of ServiceNow's tools, you'll cultivate a strong incident management process that restores services swiftly and minimizes disruption.

In the next chapter, we'll explore advanced techniques to further sharpen your incident handling skills.

Additional Resources

- **ServiceNow Documentation - Major Incident Management**
  https://docs.servicenow.com/bundle/quebec-it-service-management/page/product/major-incident-management/concept/c_MajorIncidentManagement.html
- **Best Practices for Major Incident Management**
  https://www.axelos.com/best-practice-solutions/itil

Fine-Tuning Incident Handling: Advanced Techniques

You now have a strong foundation in incident management. Let's take it to the next level and equip you with the techniques to resolve complex incidents efficiently, foster exceptional service, and ultimately elevate your IT service delivery.

The Art of Expert Troubleshooting

1. **Replicating the Issue:** Before jumping to solutions, dedicate time to accurately and reliably replicate the problem. Understand the exact steps and conditions that trigger the issue.
2. **Isolating the Cause:** Utilize a methodical approach, eliminating possibilities one by one. Consider:
   - **Recent changes:** Have any recent infrastructure changes correlated with the incident?
   - **Event logs:** Review system logs and error messages for valuable clues.
   - **Interdependencies:** Explore relationships within the CMDB – could the problem stem from related components?
3. **Leveraging Expertise Networks:** Don't hesitate to tap into the collective knowledge of your team, internal wiki, or online communities (including the ServiceNow Community forum).
4. **Hypothesis-Driven Troubleshooting:** Instead of random trial and error, form a hypothesis based on available data, test it, and refine your approach based on the results.

Advanced Incident Management Tools in ServiceNow

- **Agent Intelligence:** ServiceNow's AI-powered features present relevant knowledge articles, suggest similar incidents, and offer troubleshooting assistance, streamlining the resolution process.
- **Remote Diagnostics:** Utilize tools integrated within ServiceNow to gather configuration information, run scripts, or even remotely control a user's machine (with permission), accelerating diagnosis and resolution.
- **Debugging & Development Tools:** For incidents related to code or customizations, leverage ServiceNow's developer tools to inspect code, set breakpoints, and debug scripts.

- **Automated Remediation Actions:** Where possible, create 'Remediation Actions' within ServiceNow to automate common solutions, reducing manual effort and improving resolution speed.

Mastering "Soft Skills" within Incident Management

Technical skills are vital, but don't underestimate these skills that enhance incident handling:

- **Empathy:** Put yourself in the user's shoes. Understand their frustration and urgency through active listening and clear acknowledgment of the issue's impact.
- **Patience & Tenacity:** Complex incidents might require tenacity. Stay patient, avoid frustration, and remain focused on finding the solution.
- **Effective Communication:** Keep users informed with clear language, avoiding technical jargon. Provide regular updates, expected resolution times, and, if necessary, offer workarounds to mitigate impact.
- **Ownership:** Take responsibility for seeing an incident through even if escalations or handovers are required – ensure there is a clear owner at every step.

Shift-Left Strategies

Shift-left is a key ITSM philosophy promoting the resolution of problems as close to the user as possible, minimizing the need to escalate to specialist teams. Here's how to implement it:

- **Tier Zero** (Self-Service):
  - **Robust Knowledge Base:** Build an intuitive knowledge base filled with solutions to common issues, and actively promote its use among end users.
  - **Intelligent Virtual Agent:** Leverage AI-powered chatbots to automate the answering of basic questions and initiate self-service workflows.
- **Tier One** (Service Desk):
  - **Targeted Training:** Empower service desk agents with the tools and knowledge to resolve a broader range of incidents without escalation.
  - **Knowledge-Centered Support (KCS):** Encourage service desk agents to document resolutions and create new knowledge base articles on the fly.

The Power of Pattern Recognition

Experienced incident managers develop an eye for recurring patterns. Encourage awareness:

- **Trending and Analytics:** Analyze incident data using ServiceNow's reporting and dashboards to identify incident patterns over time. This can reveal issues prime for proactive problem management.
- **Automate Resolution of Recurring Issues:** When a pattern emerges, consider scripting or automating resolutions for frequently occurring incident categories.

Conclusion

By mastering these advanced troubleshooting techniques and tools, you'll enhance service quality and user experience. Continuously seek out opportunities for automation and shift-left initiatives to reduce incident volume and enable IT teams to focus on complex issues and proactive improvement.

In our next chapter, we'll focus on case studies and best practices to solidify your incident resolution abilities!

Additional Resources

- **ServiceNow Documentation - Agent Intelligence**
  https://docs.servicenow.com/bundle/paris-platform-user-interface/page/use/navigation/agent-intelligence.html
- **ServiceNow Blog - Shift-Left** https://blogs.servicenow.com/
- **Knowledge-Centered Support (KCS) Practices**
  https://www.servicenow.com/solutions/knowledge-management.html

Incident Resolution Strategies: Case Studies and Best Practices

Theoretical knowledge is essential; now, let's see it in action. We'll dissect incident scenarios, illustrating effective resolution strategies and reinforcing the techniques covered in previous chapters.

Case Study 1: Server Outage

- **Scenario:** Users report a critical business application as inaccessible. The website loads slowly, experiences timeouts, and is ultimately unavailable for a large user base.
- **Troubleshooting:**
    - Check event monitoring for correlated alerts (network, database, server down).
    - Examine server logs, looking for errors indicating capacity issues, hardware failure, or overload.
    - Analyze CMDB relationships to pinpoint if related components are experiencing issues.
    - Investigate recent changes, rollbacks, or patching relevant to the server or application.
- **Resolution Strategies:**
    - **Quick Fix:** If capacity is the issue, temporarily scale up server resources (if possible) to restore service immediately, buying time for a deeper solution.
    - **Restore from Backup:** In case of data corruption or configuration errors, restore a recent backup if a quick fix is not an option.
    - **Hardware Replacement:** In the case of hardware failure, initiate procurement/replacement procedures, communicating estimated timelines to users.
- **Learnings:**
    - Importance of event monitoring and the role of the CMDB in incident diagnosis.
    - Need for backup and disaster recovery plans.
    - Clear communication significantly impacts user satisfaction even during critical outages.

Case Study 2: Email Issues

- **Scenario:** A group of users report inability to send or receive external emails. Internal email communication functions normally.
- **Troubleshooting:**
  - Verify mail server status, checking for any errors or service outages.
  - Review firewall configuration and change logs to rule out recent blocks.
  - Utilize diagnostic tools (e.g., 'telnet' or 'nslookup') to test mail flow and DNS resolution.
  - Look for spam filtering issues or blacklisting – external mail providers might have blocked your domain.
- **Resolution Strategies:**
  - **Remediate Service Outage:** Restore the mail server service if an issue is found.
  - **Firewall Change:** If recent firewall changes are the cause, rectify the configuration, ensuring necessary ports and IP ranges are open.
  - **Address Blacklisting:** Contact the relevant mail provider to initiate delisting procedures.
- **Learnings:**
  - Collaboration between networking and application teams may be necessary.
  - Importance of understanding mail flow concepts for troubleshooting email-related issues.

Case Study 3: Chronic, Recurring Incident

- **Scenario:** A specific printer frequently malfunctions, impacting a department. Incidents involve paper jams, toner warnings, or inability to connect. While technicians resolve them quickly, the issue keeps recurring.
- **Troubleshooting:**
  - Analyze incident history, looking for patterns (time of occurrence, specific error types).
  - Engage closely with affected users to gather details and identify potential user error.
  - Conduct a physical inspection of the printer and its environment.
- **Resolution Strategies:**
  - **User Training:** If user error is a contributor, provide targeted training or clear instructions near the printer.

- **Preventive Maintenance:** Schedule proactive maintenance, cleaning, and part replacements.
  - **Consider Replacement:** If the printer is old, assessing the cost-benefit of replacement vs. continued repairs might be necessary.
- **Learnings:**
  - Incident trend analysis points to the need for proactive problem management.
  - Cost-benefit analysis in chronic situations guides decision-making.

Best Practices for Incident Resolution

- **Document, Document, Document:** Detailed incident resolution notes are crucial for future diagnosis of recurring issues and contribute to your knowledge base.
- **Don't Neglect the "Simple" Causes:** Explore common causes like user error, power issues, or loose cable connections, before diving into complex diagnostics.
- **Collaborate for Complex Cases:** Leverage the expertise of colleagues across various teams. A fresh perspective often aids in swift resolution.
- **Embrace the Post-Incident Review:** Especially for major or recurring incidents, hold reviews to identify recurring pain points, areas for improvement, and preventive measures.

Conclusion

By analyzing real-world situations and reinforcing best practices, you'll cultivate effective incident resolution skills. Each incident is a learning opportunity – prioritize comprehensive documentation and proactive analysis to prevent future occurrences, ultimately driving greater IT service reliability.

Next up, we'll delve into strategies to maximize incident management efficiency and effectiveness!

Additional Resources

- **Case Studies in ITIL:**
  https://www.servicenow.com/solutions/it-service-management/customer-success.html

Incident Optimization: Maximizing Efficiency and Effectiveness

Resolving incidents promptly is crucial, but true excellence lies in optimizing your process to reduce incident volume, minimize downtime, and enhance the overall user experience. Let's explore strategies and tools to achieve this.

Optimization Strategies

1. Proactive Problem Management

- **Trend Analysis:** Regularly analyze incident data using ServiceNow's reporting and analytics capabilities, identifying recurring patterns and chronic issues.
- **Trigger Problem Investigations:** Proactively initiate problem investigations when incidents repeat frequently, focusing on root cause elimination.
- **Preventing Future Outages:** Effective problem management not only solves incidents but proactively prevents them, leading to greater service stability.

2. Automation for Efficiency

- **Workflow Automation:** Analyze common incident resolution paths. If steps are repetitive and predictable, implement workflow automation. Examples:
  - Automatic system restarts for specific errors
  - Password reset workflows initiated by users via self-service portal
  - Automated hardware diagnostics or software deployment
- **Remediation Libraries:** Create a repository of scripts and automation actions used for common incident types. This streamlines resolutions and empowers lower-tier support.
- **Integrations:** Leverage integrations with monitoring, provisioning, and notification tools to automate incident creation, updates, and resolution steps where possible.

3. Shift Left and Self-Service

- **Robust Knowledge Base:** Optimize your knowledge base's search functionality, content structure, and accessibility. Aim for users to easily find solutions themselves.
- **User-Facing Knowledge Promotion:** Actively promote knowledge base use during incident communications, service portal announcements, and in training materials.

- **Intelligent Chatbots:** Utilize chatbots and virtual agents on your self-service portals. AI-powered chatbots can guide users through troubleshooting or automate the resolution of common requests.

4. Targeted Training & Skill Development

- **Upskill Service Desk:** Enhance service desk capabilities in troubleshooting recurring problems – the goal is to resolve more incidents at the first point of contact.
- **Cross-Team Training:** Conduct knowledge-sharing sessions between specialist teams and tier 1/2 support, fostering a collaborative resolution environment.
- **External Training & Certifications:** Invest in formal training or certifications (e.g., ITIL, ServiceNow certifications) to elevate your team's expertise.

Metrics for Optimization

Track the following key metrics to gauge your optimization efforts:

- **Mean Time to Resolve (MTTR):** A lower MTTR signals improved efficiency. Track average MTTRs over time.
- **Incident Volume:** Are your optimization efforts resulting in a decrease in overall incidents, especially recurring ones?
- **First Time Fix Rate:** An increasing first-time fix rate signifies better diagnostic skills and knowledge availability.
- **Self-Service & Automation Usage:** Track usage of your self-service portal, knowledge base accesses, and incidents resolved via automation for insights into shift-left success.
- **Change Success Rate:** Successful changes with no resulting incidents show improved change management practices.

Tools within ServiceNow for Optimization

- **Performance Analytics:** Provides robust reporting and dashboards to track and visualize KPIs related to incidents.
- **Workflow Editor:** ServiceNow's visual workflow editor empowers you to design and implement automation workflows.
- **Knowledge Management Module:** Manage the lifecycle of your knowledge articles, track usage, and gain insights into article effectiveness.
- **AI and Machine Learning Capabilities:** Explore ServiceNow's AI features (like 'Agent Intelligence') to assist in article suggestions and automated classification and routing.

The Role of Continual Improvement

Optimization is not a one-time project; it's an ongoing mindset:

- **Regular Reviews:** Schedule periodic reviews of incident data, processes, and metrics to identify areas in need of further improvement.
- **User Feedback:** Proactively collect user feedback through surveys or in post-closure communications, gauging satisfaction with incident resolution.
- **Knowledge Base Maintenance:** Establish a process for regularly reviewing and updating your knowledge articles to ensure information remains current and relevant.

Conclusion

By optimizing your incident management, you'll significantly reduce disruption and increase user satisfaction. Proactive prevention, leveraging automation, and a focus on continuous improvement will ensure that your IT services run at their peak.

In our next chapter, we'll delve into the fundamentals of a closely related process – Problem Management – to uncover and address the root causes behind those recurring incidents.

Additional Resources

- **ServiceNow Documentation - Performance Analytics**
  https://docs.servicenow.com/bundle/quebec-performance-analytics-and-reporting/page/use/performance-analytics/concept/pa-overview.html
- **ServiceNow Blog - 5 ways to optimize incident management**
  https://blogs.servicenow.com/

Demystifying Problem Management: Key Principles

Let's dive deep into the world of Problem Management, a process aimed at minimizing the impact of incidents and preventing them from recurring. We've learned that incident management restores service after disruptions. However, it's merely the tip of the iceberg. Problem management delves into the 'why' behind incidents and targets the root cause to reduce outages and improve the overall health of your IT infrastructure.

What is a Problem?

- A problem is an underlying cause of one or more incidents. Problems are often unknown at the time of the incident.
- Examples:
    - A faulty network switch causing multiple connectivity issues.
    - A software bug leading to application crashes.
    - Insufficient server capacity resulting in frequent slowdowns.

Difference Between Incidents and Problems

- Incidents are disruptions to service – the events users experience.
- Problems are the underlying root causes of those incidents. Think of problems as the disease, and incidents as the symptoms.

The Problem Management Process

ServiceNow's Problem Management module supports these key stages:

1. **Problem Detection and Logging**
    - **Proactive:** Incident analysis reveals recurring patterns suggesting an underlying problem. Monitoring tools might pick up systemic anomalies.
    - **Reactive:** Major incidents often warrant the creation of a linked problem for deep investigation.
2. **Investigation and Diagnosis:**
    - Technical teams delve into the root cause using troubleshooting techniques, log analysis, infrastructure examination, and often, by trying to reproduce the problem.
    - Gather information about the Configuration Items (CI) affected, recent changes, and any known errors.

3. **Workaround Identification:** While a permanent solution is being investigated, a workaround can mitigate impact, providing a temporary fix until the root cause is addressed. Document workarounds clearly.
4. **Root Cause Determination:** The goal is to establish the definitive reason behind the problem. This may involve advanced troubleshooting and analysis as outlined in an upcoming chapter on Root Cause Analysis.
5. **Resolution & Solution:**
   - **Known Error:** If the root cause is a documented issue from the vendor, a patch or update might be available.
   - **Change Request:** If the solution requires code changes, infrastructure upgrades, or configuration modifications, initiate a change request (with appropriate risk assessment).
6. **Closure:** Once the solution is implemented and thoroughly tested, the problem is closed. Thoroughly document the root cause and the resolution.

Proactive vs. Reactive Problem Management

- **Reactive Problem Management:** Initiated in response to major incidents or frequently recurring issues.
- **Proactive Problem Management:** Focuses on analyzing incident trends, performance data, and event logs to detect potential problems *before* they cause major service disruptions.

Benefits of Problem Management

- **Reduced Incident Volume:** Fewer incidents mean less disruption and improved user experience.
- **Enhanced IT Stability:** A healthy IT infrastructure free from chronic problems yields increased service reliability.
- **Cost Savings:** Preventing outages saves costs associated with downtime, support resources, and potential reputation damage.
- **Improved CSI Efforts:** Problem management drives continual service improvement initiatives by feeding into root cause analysis activities.

Problem Management Roles & Responsibilities

- **Problem Manager:** Oversees the entire problem management process, ensuring coordination between teams, and tracking progress.
- **Technical Specialists:** Conduct investigations, root cause analyses, and implement solutions depending on their area of expertise.

- **Service Desk:** Plays a crucial frontline role in identifying potential problems based on incident recurrence.
- **Change Management:** Collaborates closely with problem management to implement changes safely, aiming to resolve underlying issues.

Key Metrics for Problem Management

- **Number of Problems Resolved:** Tracks the volume of problems successfully addressed within a period.
- **Mean Time to Resolve (MTTR) for Problems:** Measures the average time it takes to resolve problems, aiding in identifying process bottlenecks.
- **Incidents Prevented:** Quantifies how proactive efforts translate into a decrease in incident volume.
- **Cost Savings:** If possible, estimates the financial benefits of downtime avoided and resources saved due to successful problem management.

Conclusion

Problem management is your secret weapon for improved service quality. Proactive prevention is far more efficient than reacting to recurring incidents. In the next chapter, we'll look at case studies and advanced techniques to enhance your problem management skills.

Additional Resources

- **ServiceNow Documentation - Problem Management**
  https://docs.servicenow.com/bundle/quebec-it-service-management/page/product/problem-management/concept/c_ProblemManagement.html

Advanced Problem Management Techniques: Case Studies

In the previous chapter, we laid the foundation for problem management. Now, we'll delve into sophisticated techniques and examine case studies that illustrate them in action.

Advanced Technique #1: Trend Analysis and Proactive Prevention

- **Going Beyond Recurring Incidents:** Problem management doesn't stop at incidents that repeat frequently. It involves analyzing broader trends to foresee potential issues.
- **Tools for Trend Identification:**
    - ServiceNow Performance Analytics: Uncover patterns on incident volume, resolution times, and incidents by category, revealing areas of potential concern.
    - System Monitoring Data: Look for anomalies in performance metrics (CPU usage, memory load, etc.) that could indicate impending failures.

Case Study: Preventing Capacity-Induced Outages

- **Scenario:** Users sporadically reported slowdowns and occasional outages of a database server, initially dismissed as minor incidents.
- **Proactive Approach:** Trend analysis revealed a steady increase in disk space usage over time and performance degradation during peak hours.
- **Preventive Action:** Instead of waiting for a major failure, the Problem Management team initiated a capacity upgrade, preemptively addressing the problem and avoiding a significant disruption.
- **Learnings:** Proactive trend analysis can pinpoint issues before they escalate into critical problems.

Advanced Technique #2: The Power of the CMDB

- **The CMDB as a Problem-Solving Tool:** Your Configuration Management Database (CMDB) is a treasure trove of information for problem investigations.
- **Visualizing Relationships:** ServiceNow's CMDB dependency maps help visualize the relationships between infrastructure components.

- **Impact Analysis:** CMDB data enables quick assessments of the potential impact of known problems and aids in prioritizing investigation efforts.

Case Study: Resolving a Network Bottleneck

- **Scenario:** Persistent latency and connection issues plagued a business-critical application, impacting multiple departments.
- **CMDB-Driven Diagnosis:** Network specialists traced the application's dependency mapping within the CMDB, revealing a specific network switch that served as a common point for impacted systems.
- **Targeted Fix:** Upon examining the switch, they found misconfigured port settings causing bottlenecks. The fix restored network performance.
- **Learnings:** The CMDB enabled a quick identification of the faulty component, minimizing troubleshooting time.

Advanced Technique #3: Structured Problem-Solving Methodologies

- **Kepner-Tregoe (K-T) Problem Analysis:** A systematic approach involving Situation Appraisal, Problem Analysis, Decision Analysis, and Potential Problem Analysis (anticipating future consequences).
- **Ishikawa Diagrams (Fishbone):** A visual tool for brainstorming potential causes, organizing them into categories like People, Process, Technology, and Environment.
- **5 Whys:** A simple but powerful technique to delve into the cause-and-effect chain by repeatedly asking 'Why?' to get to the core of an issue.

Case Study: Complex Software Bug Diagnosis

- **Scenario:** A critical software application developed in-house exhibited intermittent crashes with no obvious error messages.
- **Structured Approach:**
    - **K-T Problem Analysis:** Defined the problem, gathered data, and explored potential solutions in a structured manner.
    - **Ishikawa Diagram:** Brainstormed all potential causes across various categories.
    - **5 Whys:** Asking 'Why?' iteratively led to a discovery of a memory conflict caused by a recent third-party library update.
- **Learnings:** Structured methodologies help tackle complex problems in a more organized way.

Remember:

- **Documentation is Key:** Detailed documentation of problem descriptions, known errors, solutions, and workarounds builds a repository crucial for future diagnosis.
- **Collaboration is Essential:** Problem Management often requires the expertise of cross-functional teams. Foster a collaborative environment.
- **Continual Improvement Mindset:** Analyze the effectiveness of your problem management process and identify opportunities for refinement.

Conclusion

Advanced problem-solving techniques, combined with effective use of ServiceNow, establish proactive prevention as your ultimate goal. In the next chapter, we'll discuss a cornerstone of problem management success—root cause analysis.

Additional Resources

- **Kepner-Tregoe Problem Analysis**
  https://www.kepner-tregoe.com/problem-solving/
- **Ishikawa (Fishbone) Diagrams**
  https://asq.org/quality-resources/fishbone
- **5 Whys Technique**
  https://www.mindtools.com/pages/article/newTMC_5W.htm

Root Cause Analysis: A Comprehensive Approach

Remember that recurring incidents and major outages are usually just symptoms of a deeper problem within your IT infrastructure. Root Cause Analysis (RCA) is the methodology employed to systematically uncover the 'why' behind these problems, empowering you to fix the source issue, not just the symptoms, for lasting solutions.

What is Root Cause Analysis (RCA)?

- RCA goes beyond solving the surface issue. Its goal is to identify the fundamental reason(s) that triggered a chain of events which led to a problem or incident.
- True root causes are those that, if corrected, would prevent the problem's recurrence.

Benefits of Root Cause Analysis

- **Reduced Incident Volume:** Prevents similar incidents from happening again, saving time and resources.
- **Improved System Stability:** Robust IT environments are built on eliminating the underlying weaknesses that lead to problems.
- **Enhanced User Satisfaction:** Fewer disruptions and a more reliable service build trust in your IT capabilities.
- **Long-term Cost Savings:** Proactive problem resolution prevents the high costs associated with recurring incidents and emergency fixes.

RCA Methodologies

Let's look at some common methods used for RCA:

1. **The 5 Whys**
- A straightforward technique designed to drill down to the core cause through repeatedly asking 'Why?'.
- Example:
    - Problem: Server Crashed
    - Why? Power supply failed
    - Why? Circuit breaker tripped
    - Why? Circuit overloaded
    - Why? Recent additional equipment caused overload

- Root Cause: Insufficient circuit capacity
- Remember: The "5" in 5 Whys is flexible – sometimes you might uncover the root cause sooner, other times you may need to go deeper.

2. **Fishbone Diagrams (Ishikawa)**
- A visual approach to brainstorming and classifying potential causes into categories. Typical categories include:
  - People (human error, training)
  - Process (workflow gaps, outdated procedures)
  - Equipment (hardware failures, resource limitations)
  - Materials (software bugs, configuration issues)
  - Environment (power, network, external factors)

3. **Kepner-Tregoe (K-T) Problem Analysis**
- A more structured methodology with four distinct phases:
  - Situation Appraisal: Problem definition, data collection
  - Problem Analysis: Identify deviations, possible causes
  - Decision Analysis: Evaluate solutions, risk assessment
  - Potential Problem Analysis: Anticipate and mitigate future issues arising from the chosen solution

Conducting Root Cause Analysis: Best Practices

- **Establish a Timeline:** Record the dates, times, and sequence of events leading up to the incident or problem.
- **Preserve the Evidence:** Avoid making immediate changes that might erase valuable clues – take snapshots and configuration backups where possible.
- **Gather Data:** Include event logs, configuration settings, monitoring data, user reports, and recent change records.
- **Involve the Right People:** Collaborate with relevant technical teams, and even vendors or external partners if needed.
- **Facilitate Open Discussions:** Create a safe environment for blameless brainstorming to encourage honest information sharing.

The Role of ServiceNow in RCA

ServiceNow supports your RCA process:

- **Incident and Problem Records:** Detailed documentation is built-in, including associated changes, workarounds, and resolution notes.
- **CMDB:** Provides insights into infrastructure relationships.
- **Analytics and Reporting:** Helps identify trends and patterns potentially hinting at systemic root causes.

The Importance of Documentation

- **Thorough Root Cause Description:** Document the identified root cause(s) clearly and concisely on the problem record.
- **Lessons Learned:** Capture insights, decision-making processes, and the rationale for chosen solutions. This creates a valuable knowledge base to prevent recurrence.

Beyond Fixing: Continual Improvement

RCA should feed into your broader improvement initiatives:

- **Problem Management Trend Analysis:** Look for patterns across root causes for areas requiring deeper focus.
- **Change Management Reviews:** If implemented solutions cause new issues, review your change management practices.
- **Knowledge Base Enrichment:** Add insights from RCA into your knowledge articles, making the information more valuable and actionable.

Conclusion

RCA is a powerful tool, but it takes practice. Start with smaller problems to build your skills. Focus on accurate documentation and leverage the insights from RCA to drive your IT service delivery to a new level of stability.

In the next chapter, we'll discuss practical strategies to implement solutions successfully and restore normal operations.

Additional Resources

- **The 5 Whys Technique**
  https://www.mindtools.com/pages/article/newTMC_5W.htm
- **Fishbone Diagram** https://asq.org/quality-resources/fishbone
- **Kepner-Tregoe Problem Analysis**
  https://www.kepner-tregoe.com/problem-solving/

Problem Resolution Strategies: Implementing Solutions

After meticulous investigation and root cause identification, it's time for the next stage in the Problem Management process: finding and implementing the right fix. This chapter covers effective problem resolution strategies, the crucial link between Change Management, knowledge updates, and ensuring your solutions restore stability.

Strategies for Finding the Right Solution

1. **Known Error Database (KEDB):**
   - Start by exploring vendor-provided KEDBs for your software or hardware components. Solutions or patches for known issues might already exist.
2. **Internal Knowledge Base:**
   - Review your own knowledge base for solutions applied to past similar problems. This leverages your team's collective experience.
3. **Expert Consultation:**
   - Engage internal Subject Matter Experts (SMEs) or external vendors/consultants specializing in the specific technology.
4. **Internet Research:**
   - Search online forums, vendor documentation, and technical blogs. Communities often offer valuable advice for known problems.
5. **Vendor Support:**
   - If all else fails, open a support ticket with the relevant vendor. Provide the detailed results of your root cause analysis.

Change Management: The Key to Controlled Implementation

Significant problem resolutions nearly always require changes to your IT infrastructure. Collaborate with your Change Management team:

- **Risk Assessment:** Thoroughly assess potential risks and impacts of the solution, prioritize changes based on risk levels.
- **Scheduling and Planning:** Coordinate change implementation in a way that minimizes disruption and aligns with your change windows.

- **Testing:** Implement the solution in a testing environment first, whenever possible, to validate the fix and identify unforeseen side effects.
- **Change Documentation:** Maintain comprehensive change records including the problem it addresses, solution details, testing outcomes, and back-out plans.

The Importance of Workarounds (And Avoiding Them!)

- **When Workarounds Are Necessary:** For problems requiring lengthy fixes, a temporary workaround may be essential to mitigate impact.
- **Document Rigorously:** Clearly document workarounds, including known limitations and steps for removal once a permanent solution is in place.
- **The Temporary Trap:** Don't let workarounds become permanent. Actively track problems with workarounds, ensuring focus remains on a long-term solution.

Implementation Best Practices

- **Communication Is Key:** Inform stakeholders about the planned fix, estimated timelines, potential impact, and how they will be notified once the solution is in place.
- **Pilot Approach:** Where feasible, roll out solutions to a smaller group of users or a subset of infrastructure first. This helps catch unexpected issues before broader implementation.
- **Monitoring and Verification:** After implementation, thoroughly monitor affected systems to ensure the problem is fully resolved and no new issues have arisen.
- **Back-out Plan:** Have a well-defined back-out plan ready in case the solution leads to instability or complications.

Updating Your Knowledge Base

Knowledge-sharing is vital to prevent the recurrence of issues and speed up future resolutions:

- **Problem Resolution Notes:** Enrich problem records with a detailed description of the solution, steps taken, and results achieved.
- **New Knowledge Articles:** If the solution isn't documented already, create a new article for your knowledge base. Clearly link it to the problem record.

- **Share Successes:** Highlight effective solutions in team meetings or internal newsletters to foster a learning culture.

Problem Closure and Review

Once the problem is resolved:

1. **Verification:** Get confirmation from users and stakeholders that the issue appears fixed. Conduct comprehensive testing.
2. **Closure:** Formally close the problem record in ServiceNow, documenting the solution and outcome.
3. **Post-Implementation Review:** Especially for complex fixes or those with initial uncertainty, schedule a review to assess the solution's effectiveness and identify potential improvement areas.

ServiceNow Tools to Support Your Journey

- **Problem Record:** The central hub for documenting the problem, root cause, solution, and link it to change records.
- **Change Management Module:** Seamlessly create changes directly from problem records, ensuring controlled implementation.
- **Knowledge Base:** Capture, share, and improve valuable problem resolution knowledge across your IT organization.

Conclusion

Successful problem resolution delivers lasting improvements to service stability. By effectively collaborating with Change Management, updating your knowledge base, and communicating transparently, you'll transform those hard-earned insights into a more reliable IT environment.

Next up, let's turn our focus to another core ITSM process: Request Fulfillment!

Additional Resources

- **ServiceNow Documentation - Change Management**
  https://docs.servicenow.com/bundle/quebec-it-service-management/page/product/change-management/concept/c_ChangeManagement.html
- **Best Practices for IT Change Management**
  https://www.atlassian.com/itsm/change-management/best-practices

Streamlining Request Fulfillment: Essential Concepts

While incidents focus on unplanned disruptions, request fulfillment handles the predictable needs of users – from new hardware or software access to account resets and onboarding tasks. An efficient request fulfillment process ensures timely delivery and is key to customer satisfaction.

What is a Service Request?

- A service request is a user-initiated formal request for something to be provided. Often these are based on pre-defined options within a service catalog.
- Examples:
  - Password resets
  - Access to a shared drive
  - New laptop provisioning
  - Software installations
  - Employee onboarding/offboarding tasks

The Request Fulfillment Process

Let's break down the key stages within ServiceNow's Request Fulfillment module:

1. **Initiation:**
   - **User-friendly Service Catalog:** Present users with a clear, intuitive catalog of standard services they can request (more on this later).
   - **Request Forms:** Provide well-structured forms that capture all necessary information for the specific request type.
2. **Approval (if necessary):**
   - **Automated Approvals:** For simple, low-risk requests, configure automated approval workflows to reduce delays.
   - **Approver Routing:** Define approval chains based on the cost, complexity, or business policies associated with different request types.
3. **Fulfillment:**
   - **Task Creation:** Break down the request into tasks assigned to relevant teams or individuals (e.g., hardware team, software deployment team, etc.).

- ○ **Workflows and Automation:** Utilize ServiceNow's workflow engine to automate repetitive manual steps within request fulfillment.
- ○ **Coordination:** Coordinate activities involved in fulfilling the request seamlessly. This may involve multiple teams, vendors, or procurements.

4. **Closure:**
   - ○ **User Verification:** Notify the user once the request is completed and confirm their satisfaction.
   - ○ **Record Keeping:** Maintain closed request records for reporting, audit, and knowledge base building.

The Foundation: A Well-Designed Service Catalog

Your service catalog is the user-facing storefront of your request process. Focus on:

- **Intuitive Structure:** Organize your catalog into logical categories that make sense to users, not your internal IT structure.
- **Clarity and Conciseness:** Descriptions of services should be non-technical with clear explanations of what the user will receive.
- **Variable Design:** Use form fields intelligently to gather the right information, minimizing back-and-forth with the user (e.g., for hardware, have dropdowns for model selections rather than free text).
- **Search Integration:** A robust search function helps users quickly find what they need within your catalog.

Types of Service Requests

- **Standard Requests:** Pre-defined, common requests with established fulfillment procedures (e.g., new employee setup).
- **Access Requests:** Granting or revoking access to applications, systems, or data (often linked to approvals).
- **Provisioning Requests:** Provisioning hardware, software licenses, or setting up user accounts.
- **Information Requests:** Requests for reports, data extracts, or specific knowledge from the team.

Key Metrics for Request Fulfillment

Track these to measure your efficiency:

- **Fulfillment Time:** Average time from request submission to completion.

- **First-Level Resolution Rate:** Percentage of requests resolved without needing escalation to higher-tier specialists.
- **Backlog Volume:** Monitor open requests to avoid bottlenecks.
- **User Satisfaction:** Gather feedback through surveys to gauge how satisfied users are with the process.

ServiceNow Tools to Optimize Request Fulfillment

- **Service Catalog Builder:** Visually design your catalog, request forms, and workflows.
- **Approval Rules Engine:** Set up approval logic based on various criteria.
- **Task Management:** Manage task assignment, tracking, and updates efficiently.
- **Reporting and Dashboards:** Track metrics, analyze trends, and identify areas for improvement.

Conclusion

A streamlined request fulfillment process significantly improves the user experience and frees up IT resources from repetitive tasks. In the next chapter, we'll discuss how to optimize the process even further, enhancing productivity and delighting your users.

Additional Resources

- **ServiceNow Documentation - Service Catalog Management**
  https://docs.servicenow.com/bundle/quebec-it-service-management/page/product/service-catalog-management/concept/c_ServiceCatalogManagement.html

Optimizing Request Fulfillment: Practical Approaches

In this chapter, we'll explore practical optimization techniques to boost efficiency, cut down wait times, and enhance the overall user experience. Building on the foundation laid in the previous chapter, it's time to take your request fulfillment to even greater heights.

1. Automation: Your Efficiency Superpower

- **Identify Repetitive Tasks:** Analyze your requests. Are there steps that are always the same (password resets, standard software installs, simple access requests)? These are prime candidates for automation.
- **Workflows for the Win:** Use ServiceNow's workflow engine to automatically: * Assign tasks based on request type * Trigger email notifications to stakeholders * Provision simple resources (like adding a user to a distribution group) * Run scripts to streamline multi-step processes
- **Pre-Approved Requests:** For low-risk standard requests, automate the entire process, including approval.

2. Shift Left with Self-Service Refinements

- **Robust Service Catalog:** Continuously adjust your catalog for clarity. Review search terms users enter, identify what they struggle to find, and refine your structure or descriptions.
- **Intelligent Knowledge Base Integration:** Link relevant knowledge articles directly in your request forms. This can offer solutions for common issues, potentially deflecting the need to submit a request in the first place.
- **Request Templates:** Provide pre-filled request templates, especially for more complex or recurring requests. This speeds up submission for users and ensures your team gets the right information.
- **Virtual Agent for Assistance:** Deploy ServiceNow's virtual agent (chatbot) to guide users through the request process, answer basic questions, or even automate standard requests.

3. The Power of Proactive Fulfilment

- **Event-Triggered Fulfillment:** Integrate your monitoring tools with ServiceNow. Create automated workflows to proactively fulfill requests based on specific events.

○ Example: Low disk space alert triggers a storage upgrade request

- **Anticipating User Needs:** Analyze user roles and onboarding processes. Can standard software or access configurations be provisioned *before* a new employee even starts?
- **Regularly Review Catalog:** Is your catalog up to date? Do new IT services or offerings need to be added? Stale catalogs create friction.

4. Prioritization for Optimal Resource Allocation

- **Clearly Define Priorities:** Establish a clear prioritization matrix (e.g., 'Critical,' 'High,' 'Medium,' 'Low') based on impact and urgency. Communicate this to users.
- **Prioritized Queues:** Within ServiceNow, assign requests to different queues based on their priority. This helps teams focus on the most critical tasks first.
- **Dynamic Prioritization:** Can external factors influence priority? Configure dynamic updates (e.g., if an executive submits a request, it may be marked higher priority). *Use this sparingly*.

5. Communication and Transparency

- **Proactive Status Updates:** Let users know where things stand. Automated email notifications at key stages (submitted, approved, in progress, fulfilled) reduce inbound "status check" inquiries.
- **Estimated Completion Times:** Where possible, set expectations. Even a rough estimate ("requests like this usually take 2 business days") is better than none.
- **Self-Service Tracking:** Allow users to track their request status via the portal, reducing calls to the service desk asking for updates.

Tools within ServiceNow to Elevate Optimization

- **Workflow Orchestrator:** Design and implement complex automation workflows with ease.
- **Integration Hub:** Explore pre-built integrations with monitoring, provisioning, or other tools in your IT landscape.
- **Performance Analytics:** Analyze request data to spot bottlenecks, identify automation opportunities, and track improvement over time.
- **Virtual Agent:** Create conversational AI-powered chatbot interactions.

The Importance of Measurement and Feedback

- **Track Your KPIs:** Regularly assess the metrics discussed in the previous chapter to identify the impact of your optimization efforts.
- **User Feedback Surveys:** Proactively gather feedback on request satisfaction. Did users find what they needed easily? Were they happy with the turnaround time?
- **Continuous Improvement Loop:** Use this data to drive further refinements to your service catalog, workflows, and knowledge base.

Conclusion

Optimized request fulfillment delivers a satisfying user experience and frees up precious IT resources. The key is continuous refinement. Track your metrics, embrace automation opportunities, and prioritize user-centric improvements.

Next, we'll discuss ways to make your request management process even more successful!

Additional Resources

- **ServiceNow Documentation - Workflow Automation**
  https://docs.servicenow.com/bundle/quebec-servicenow-platform/page/build/workflow/concept/c_Workflow.html
- **ServiceNow Documentation - Integrations**
  https://docs.servicenow.com/bundle/paris-application-development/page/integrate/integration-landing-page.html

Enhancing Request Management: Strategies for Success

Let's take your request process beyond the efficient fulfillment we've discussed into the realm of delivering exceptional service. In this chapter, we'll focus on strategies to create a truly delightful and user-centric request management experience. While optimization improves efficiency, true enhancement is about fostering a positive relationship between IT and your users. Let's explore how to achieve this and boost customer satisfaction.

Strategy 1: Building a User-First Culture

- **Empathy as a Core Value:** Emphasize understanding the needs, frustrations, and time constraints of your users. Proactive communication, avoiding jargon, and aiming for first-time resolution all reinforce this approach.
- **"Customer-First" Mindset in IT:** Shift the perception of IT from a reactive fix-it shop to a proactive service provider focused on enabling the business. This impacts everything from catalog design to communication style.
- **Gather User Insights:** Collect regular user feedback on their experience. Use a combination of surveys, focus groups, and informal conversations to understand the user's perspective.

Strategy 2: Promoting Your Service Catalog

Your beautifully designed catalog is useless if no one knows about it. Consider these approaches:

- **Intranet Promotion:** Create a prominent banner or featured spot on your company intranet, especially during employee onboarding.
- **Targeted Announcements:** When new services are added to your catalog, send announcements to the relevant departments or user groups.
- **Inclusion in Training Materials:** Make the service catalog a standard part of IT onboarding for managers and new employees.
- **Lunch and Learn Sessions:** Hold informal sessions to demonstrate to users the value of the catalog and how to use it effectively.

Strategy 3: The Power of Proactive Communication

- **Clarity is Key:** Don't just tell users their request is in progress. If there's a backlog or external dependency, let them know with an explanation and a revised ETA.
- **Address Potential Delays Quickly:** If something causes a delay, inform the user, reset the expectations, and offer alternatives if possible.
- **Major Disruptions:** If a service relied on in many requests is down, create a banner for your catalog or send a proactive alert to prevent an influx of duplicate requests.

Strategy 4: Request Management Beyond the Ticket

- **The Relationship Factor:** Especially for requests with long lead times (e.g., onboarding), assign a point of contact. This builds trust and facilitates two-way communication.
- **Self-Service Tracking:** Enable users to see not just their request status, but the steps involved, clarifying where in the process things are.
- **Offering Alternatives:** If a user's request can't be fulfilled as asked, don't just say no. Guide them to potential workarounds or alternative options.

Strategy 5: Leveraging Data for Insights

- **Request Trend Analysis:** Analyze your request data. Are there surges at specific times of the year? This helps with capacity planning and pre-emptive measures.
- **Identifying Automation Potential:** Which requests generate high volume but are repetitive and low complexity? Target these first for automation.
- **Data-Driven Catalog Refinement:** Are there frequently requested items not in the catalog? Are there outdated catalog items that never get used?

ServiceNow Features to Aid Enhancement

- **Surveys:** Utilize ServiceNow's survey capabilities to gather structured user feedback for continuous improvement.
- **Reporting and Dashboards:** Visualize request trends, identify patterns in user behavior, and monitor request satisfaction metrics.
- **Notifications:** Configure targeted notifications to keep users informed and to proactively address potential delays or issues.

- **User Criteria:** Consider using user criteria for dynamic assignment, ensuring complex requests are routed to experienced staff.

Continuous Improvement for Exceptional Service

- **Celebrate Successes:** When you get stellar feedback from users, showcase it to your team. This builds pride and reinforces the value of a customer-centric approach.
- **Regular Reviews:** Analyze your process, metrics, and user feedback on a regular cadence. Proactively make adjustments to refine your approach.

Conclusion

Exceptional request management solidifies IT's role as a trusted business partner. By embedding a user-first mindset, proactively communicating, and leveraging insights from data, you'll cultivate a positive, productive, and frictionless experience for your users.

Up next, let's dive into the fundamental ITIL process of Change Management and how ServiceNow streamlines its implementation!

Additional Resources

- **ITSM Best Practices – Request Fulfillment**
  https://www.servicenow.com/solutions/request-management.html

Transformative Change Management: Fundamentals and Strategies

Let's explore the strategic and structured approach that is Change Management. This crucial process protects service stability when changes to your IT infrastructure are necessary. Change is the lifeblood of IT. New technologies, updated systems, evolving business needs – these all necessitate changes. Effective Change Management aims to implement changes with minimal disruption to your users and services, and maximum success rates.

What is a Change in ITSM?

A change is any modification to a Configuration Item (CI) that can impact an IT service. CIs include hardware, software, infrastructure, processes, or documentation. Examples of changes include:

- Software upgrades or patches
- Hardware replacements or installations
- Firewall configuration modifications
- Data center migrations
- New process rollouts (even if no technology element is involved)

The Role of Change Management

- **Risk Reduction:** A structured process helps assess the potential impact of a change, ensuring necessary precautions are taken.
- **Minimizing Disruption:** Change Management focuses on scheduling, communication, and thorough testing to prevent outages.
- **Improving Success Rates:** Pre-approval reviews, back-out plans, and post-implementation checks lead to a higher overall success rate of change implementation.
- **Compliance & Auditability:** Detailed records support compliance requirements and aid in future analysis if changes lead to problems.

The Change Management Process

ServiceNow's Change Management module supports these key stages:

1. **Request Submission:**
   - Well-defined change forms capture all relevant details: reason, scope, impact, urgency, risk assessment, and a detailed implementation plan.

2. **Review and Approval:**
   - ○ Establish the Change Advisory Board (CAB) - a cross-functional decision-making body.
   - ○ CAB reviews and approves changes based on risk, aligning with any priority matrices.
3. **Planning and Scheduling:**
   - ○ Coordinate implementation, aligning with maintenance windows
   - ○ Plan for resource allocation, testing, and clear communication
   - ○ Build a detailed back-out plan.
4. **Implementation:**
   - ○ Follow the implementation plan meticulously.
   - ○ Thoroughly document every step taken.
5. **Review and Closure:**
   - ○ Conduct a post-implementation review to assess the change's success.
   - ○ Capture lessons learned for future changes.

Types of Changes

- **Standard Changes:** Low-risk, pre-approved, routine changes with well-established procedures (e.g., some password resets, standard software deployments).
- **Normal Changes:** Require CAB assessment, approval, and follow the standard change process.
- **Emergency Changes:** Address urgent issues, may have an expedited approval process, but still must adhere to as much process as possible, with rigorous documentation.

Change Management Success Factors

- **Clear Roles & Responsibilities:** Define who the change initiator, the approvers (CAB), implementers, and stakeholders are.
- **Communication & Transparency:** Inform users in advance about planned changes. For unplanned outages, have a clear communication process to broadcast updates and ETAs.
- **CI Baseline Knowledge:** Your CMDB is crucial for effective impact assessment – know what you have and how it's connected.
- **Collaboration:** Change Management works best when IT teams work together throughout the process.

ServiceNow Tools to Support Change Management

- **Change Request Forms:** Customizable forms ensure necessary information is captured.
- **Approval Workflows:** Automate routing to the appropriate CAB members based on change type.
- **Change Calendar:** Visualize upcoming changes for planning, avoiding conflicts, and identifying potential bottlenecks.
- **Reporting:** Track change success rates, volume, and identify trends to improve.

Conclusion

Change Management protects IT service health while driving progress. Embrace a structured approach, emphasize communication, and leverage ServiceNow features for a streamlined, reliable change process.

In our next chapter, we'll delve into the finer points of change management for maximum efficiency and success!

Additional Resources

- **ServiceNow Documentation - Change Management**
  https://docs.servicenow.com/bundle/quebec-it-service-management/page/product/change-management/concept/c_ChangeManagement.html

Change Management Mastery: Implementation Techniques

Let's get into the nitty-gritty of how to execute successful change initiatives with minimal disruption. In this chapter, we'll cover techniques to streamline implementation, foster collaboration, and mitigate risks. Building on the foundation laid in the previous chapter, let's explore how to turn your change process into a well-oiled machine for smooth IT transformations.

Technique 1: The Change Advisory Board (CAB)

- **Diverse Membership:** Include representatives from different IT teams (infrastructure, applications, development), and potentially even key business stakeholders.
- **Defined Decision-making:** Is approval by consensus, majority vote, or does a specific member have veto power? Make this clear upfront.
- **CAB Meetings:** Regular CAB meetings ensure timely review and discussion of change requests. ServiceNow can automate calendar invites and reminders.
- **Emergency CAB:** For urgent changes, have a smaller, empowered group authorized to make rapid decisions as needed.

Technique 2: Change Models & Templates

- **Standardize:** Develop templates for change requests that mandate the necessary information for proper assessment.
- **Pre-Approved Changes:** Identify a set of low-risk, routine changes (standard changes), and automate their approval for maximum efficiency.
- **Workflows:** Utilize ServiceNow workflow capabilities to map out the different paths change requests can take based on type, risk level, and approval chains.

Technique 3: Thorough Planning and Testing

- **Robust Implementation Plans:** Every change request should have a step-by-step plan, including resource requirements, dependencies, and testing.
- **Testing Environments:** Mimic changes in a test environment whenever possible, especially for complex changes with high potential impact.

- **Back-out Plans:** Develop detailed back-out plans for every change. The act of planning for reversal forces you to think through scenarios that might go wrong.

Technique 4: Effective Communication

- **Change Calendar:** Maintain a visible change calendar with planned dates and brief descriptions. Users can self-serve, reducing inquiries.
- **Targeted Notifications:** Use ServiceNow's notification features to send alerts about changes relevant to specific user groups (e.g., email system going down for brief maintenance).
- **Unplanned Outages:** For major disruptions outside of scheduled changes, establish a rapid communication protocol using channels like SMS, company intranet banners, or dedicated status pages.

Technique 5: Post-Implementation Review (PIR)

- **Mandatory Step:** Make PIRs a non-negotiable part of your change closure process. Schedule a brief review meeting shortly after implementation.
- **Lessons Learned:** Focus on what worked well, what didn't, and how to improve the process. Update your documentation with these insights.
- **Data-Driven Improvement:** Utilize ServiceNow reporting to track change success rates, common reasons for failure, and trends over time.

ServiceNow Tools to Optimize Implementation

- **Change Schedule View (Calendar):** Visualize and manage upcoming changes.
- **Automated Approval Workflows:** Eliminate manual bottlenecks and speed up the process through automated routing.
- **Task Management:** Break changes into tasks, track progress, and coordinate teams effectively.
- **Integration with Monitoring Tools:** Trigger actions or updates based on real-time monitoring data for a more dynamic approach.

Continuous Improvement for Change Management Excellence

- **Change Management Metrics:** Monitor success rates, volume, lead times, and adherence to change windows. Use this data to identify process improvement areas.

- **Regular CAB Reviews:** The CAB should periodically review the overall change management process and make adjustments to improve efficiency and agility.
- **Reward Success:** Acknowledge teams and individuals involved in successful changes. This reinforces the value of a disciplined change management approach.

Conclusion

Mastering Change Management empowers IT to drive innovation. By ensuring structured assessment, meticulous planning, effective communication, and a focus on continuous improvement, you'll maximize stability while delivering essential updates and improvements.

In the next chapter, we'll discuss ways to approach and overcome common challenges in Change Management.

Additional Resources

- **Best Practices for Change Management Communication**
  https://www.servicenow.com/solutions/change-management.html

Navigating Change Challenges: Advanced Approaches

Let's get ready to tackle the inevitable bumps in the road of Change Management. This chapter focuses on advanced strategies for overcoming common hurdles and ensuring the success of your changes. Even the best-laid change plans can face obstacles. Being aware of common challenges allows you to plan preemptive mitigation strategies for a smoother process.

Challenge 1: Resistance to Change

- **Understanding Resistance:** Change disrupts familiar routines. Some resistance is natural. Proactively address fears, potential skill gaps, and workload concerns.
- **Communication is Key:** Emphasize the 'why' behind the change, and the benefits it brings to users or the business as a whole.
- **Champions for Change:** Identify early adopters within different teams or user groups. Their enthusiasm can be infectious.
- **Training and Support:** Provide training well in advance of the change for any impacted users, ensuring they feel comfortable with the new process or feature.

Challenge 2: Conflicts in Scheduling

- **Change Windows:** Clearly define maintenance windows, and communicate them widely. Negotiate with stakeholders if necessary.
- **Change Freeze Periods:** For peak business times (e.g., retailers during the holiday season), consider implementing 'change freezes' to minimize risk.
- **Resource Contention:** Plan thoroughly, ensuring resources (people, systems) needed for a change aren't already overbooked. Visualizing changes in the calendar view is key.
- **Dependency Awareness:** Your CMDB is invaluable here. Understand dependencies between services, and schedule changes in a way that minimizes cascading incidents.

Challenge 3: Unforeseen Issues & Scope Creep

- **Thorough Testing:** Testing in a staging environment helps uncover potential problems before they impact your production environment.

- **Contingency Plans:** Even with the best planning, things can go wrong. Have back-out plans and clearly define roll-back procedures.
- **Scope Management:** Resist the urge to add to the change mid-implementation. Document additional requests, and assess them for a future change cycle.
- **Agile Mindset:** Where appropriate, break large changes into smaller chunks. This can manage complexity, and make it easier to adapt if needed.

Challenge 4: Lack of Collaboration and Buy-in

- **Cross-Functional CAB:** CAB membership including different IT teams ensures all aspects of a change are assessed for potential impact.
- **Business Stakeholders:** When changes heavily impact business users, involve them early on for input and to secure buy-in.
- **Transparency Builds Trust:** Sharing change successes and failures openly fosters a culture where change management isn't seen as a blocker, but an efficiency enabler.

Challenge 5: Ineffective Post-Change Analysis

- **Mandatory PIRs:** Post-Implementation Reviews are too often skipped. Make them standard practice, even for seemingly minor successful changes.
- **Celebrate Success:** Acknowledge successful changes, the teams involved, and the role the process played. This reinforces its value.
- **Honest Evaluation of Failures:** When things don't go smoothly, focus on root cause analysis - avoid blame games. The lessons learned are invaluable.

ServiceNow Tools to Overcome Challenges

- **Change Calendar:** Helps in identifying scheduling conflicts and potential resource bottlenecks.
- **CMDB Dependency Mapping:** Visualizes how a change might cascade to other parts of your infrastructure.
- **Post-Implementation Review (PIR):** Provides a structured framework for capturing lessons learned during change implementation.
- **Reporting & Analytics:** Identifies recurring issues, helping to target process improvements.

Don't Become Complacent

- **Metrics Matter:** Regular tracking of change success rates, lead times, and adherence to change windows can help you spot trends and address challenges as they arise.
- **User Feedback:** Proactively survey users post-change to gauge satisfaction and identify points of friction.
- **Never Stop Learning:** Change Management is an ongoing process. Stay up-to-date on best practices, and continuously refine your approach.

Conclusion

Successfully navigating change challenges establishes IT as a change catalyst rather than a roadblock. By anticipating challenges, emphasizing communication, and utilizing the tools within ServiceNow, your IT organization will pave the way for innovation and successful transformations.

Next up, let's discuss how to sustain your Change Management achievements in the long term to support ongoing IT excellence.

Additional Resources

- **Overcoming Resistance to Change in IT**
  https://www.cio.com/article/2383581/it-strategy/7-tips-for-overcoming-resistance-to-change-in-it.html
- **Change Management Best Practices**
  https://www.servicenow.com/solutions/change-management.html

Sustaining Change Success: Continuous Improvement Strategies

In this chapter, we'll focus on ensuring your successful changes don't unravel over time, and discuss embedding continuous improvement into your processes. Implementing successful changes is an important step, but sustaining that success and driving continuous improvement is where true value lies for your IT organization.

Strategy 1: Reinforcing the Value of Change Management

- **Wins Need Visibility:** Don't just track change successes internally. Regularly share key wins with stakeholders (e.g., reduced unplanned outages due to upgrades, faster service delivery enabled by new changes).
- **Measure the Benefits:** Where possible, go beyond 'success rates.' Quantify the impact of changes (time saved, costs reduced, user satisfaction scores).
- **Celebrate Teamwork:** Acknowledge teams who collaborate seamlessly on change implementation, making the process itself a point of pride.

Strategy 2: Knowledge Management: The Key to Consistency

- **Documentation as a Discipline:** Detailed records of past changes, decisions, and outcomes are essential for future diagnosis and learning.
- **Centralized Knowledge Base:** Make sure this knowledge is easily searchable and accessible across the IT organization. ServiceNow's Knowledge Management module is your ally.
- **Link Changes to KB Articles:** For troubleshooting, having change records directly connected to relevant knowledge empowers your teams.
- **Knowledge Ownership:** Promote a culture of updating and sharing knowledge, ensuring your KB isn't just an archive, but a living resource.

Strategy 3: Proactive Change Reviews

- **Scheduled Change Audits:** Regularly review closed change records to assess if they truly achieved their objectives, and if implementations are running smoothly over time.
- **Recurring Issues:** Are the same problems continually addressed with repeated, similar changes? This signals a need for deeper problem management.

- **Evolving the CAB Agenda:** As your IT environment and business needs change, the CAB should periodically review its assessment criteria and risk models.

Strategy 4: Change Management as a Learning Process

- **Post-Implementation Reviews (PIRs):** Make PIRs mandatory, focusing not just on what went right or wrong, but why. Document insights for future changes.
- **Feedback Loops:** Gather user feedback after changes. Did it solve intended problems? Create any new ones? This can highlight process blind spots.
- **External Trends:** Stay informed on broader change management best practices. Frameworks like ITIL are constantly evolving – embrace learning.

Strategy 5: Continuous Improvement Mindset

- **Data is Your Friend:** ServiceNow analytics helps you spot positive and negative trends in your change process. Is approval time slowing down? Why?
- **Small Improvements Matter:** Not every optimization requires a massive overhaul. Incremental refinements reinforce a culture of progress.
- **Adaptation is Key:** IT systems and business needs change; so should your process. Don't let your Change Management approach stagnate.

ServiceNow Tools to Support Your Journey

- **Reporting & Dashboards:** Visualize change metrics, success rates, identify bottlenecks, and track progress over time.
- **CMDB:** A robust CMDB enables analysis of the long-term impact of changes on your infrastructure.
- **Knowledge Base:** Easily link changes to KB articles for future reference, ensuring knowledge retention.
- **Surveys:** Gather structured change feedback from users and stakeholders to identify areas for improvement.

The Importance of Celebrating Milestones

- **Small Wins Matter:** Don't just focus on major project success – acknowledge smaller process improvements as well.

- **Recognizing the Team:** Builds motivation. Highlight those who consistently champion adherence to process, suggest refinements, or share valuable insights during PIRs.
- **Sharing Successes:** Brief company-wide announcements or spotlights in team meetings reinforce the role IT plays in enabling change rather than blocking it.

Conclusion

Sustaining change success is not a one-time activity. By prioritizing knowledge sharing, conducting regular reviews, and embracing a mindset of continuous improvement, you'll transform Change Management into a core enabler of IT-driven innovation.

In our next chapter, we'll begin exploring another cornerstone of ITSM: the value of a robust Configuration Management Database (CMDB).

Additional Resources

- **Benefits of Continuous Improvement in IT**
  https://www.cio.com/article/2383521/it-strategy/5-ways-to-encourage-continuous-improvement-in-it.html
- **How to Build a Continual Improvement Culture**
  https://hbr.org/2012/11/building-a-culture-of-continuous-improvement

Unveiling the Power of CMDB: Core Concepts and Applications

This chapter will unveil the power of a well-maintained Configuration Management Database (CMDB) and how it elevates numerous ITSM processes. Think of your CMDB as the digital blueprint of your entire IT environment. It's a centralized repository that goes far beyond simple asset tracking, and is the backbone of informed decision-making.

What is a CMDB?

- **Configuration Items (CIs):** The building blocks of your CMDB. CIs include hardware (servers, laptops), software (applications, databases), network devices, documentation, cloud services, and even people or teams.
- **Relationships:** The magic of the CMDB lies in mapping relationships between CIs. This visualizes dependencies, allowing for a deep understanding of your IT landscape.
- **Attributes** CIs store a wealth of data: serial numbers, licensing information, configuration settings, owners, support teams, location, and more.

Key Concepts

- **Accuracy is Paramount:** Your CMDB is only as powerful as the data it holds. Inaccurate or outdated information leads to poor decisions.
- **Federation vs. Consolidation:** Some organizations opt for federated CMDBs (spread across tools) with ServiceNow acting as an aggregator. Others aim for full consolidation within ServiceNow for a 'single source of truth.'
- **The Power of Visualization:** CMDBs offer dependency maps. These graphical representations unlock a deeper understanding of how your IT infrastructure is connected.

Why Does Your CMDB Matter?

Let's explore core applications across your ITSM processes:

1. **Incident & Problem Management**
   - **Faster Troubleshooting:** Quickly see what other CIs or services might be affected during an outage, reducing diagnostic time.

- **Impact Analysis:** Proactively assess the potential impact of a problem on dependent services.
- **Repeat Incident Spotting:** Identify if a CI is involved in recurring issues, signaling a deeper problem to tackle.

2. **Change Management**
   - **Risk Reduction:** See all CIs and their dependencies that a change might impact, enabling more thorough pre-change analysis.
   - **Collision Prevention:** Visually spot if changes to different CIs are scheduled for the same time window, potentially causing conflicts.
   - **Post-Implementation Verification:** Check if a change was implemented as intended by comparing the CMDB's 'before' and 'after' state.

3. **Request Fulfilment**
   - **Software Licensing:** Ensure sufficient software licenses are available before provisioning new instances or granting access.
   - **Capacity Management:** Is there enough server capacity, storage, or network bandwidth to handle the requested new service?
   - **User Context:** See a user's existing devices and installed software configurations to assist with their requests efficiently.

4. **Knowledge Management**
   - **Targeted Knowledge:** Link knowledge base articles directly to relevant CIs, so the right information is at hand during troubleshooting.
   - **Vulnerability Alerts:** If a known vulnerability is associated with a CI in your CMDB, proactively target knowledge and solutions to affected teams.

CMDB Best Practices

- **Define Your Scope:** Not everything needs to be a CI. Focus on CIs essential for service delivery and decision making.
- **Ownership & Governance:** Clear data ownership is crucial. Who is responsible for maintaining the accuracy of different CI types?
- **Automated Discovery:** Utilize ServiceNow Discovery and integrations with monitoring tools to populate and update your CMDB, reducing manual effort.
- **Data Integrity Checks:** Regular audits and reconciliation processes ensure the CMDB reflects reality and can be trusted.

ServiceNow: Your CMDB Powerhouse

- **Discovery & Mapping:** Discover CIs across your network, on-premises, and in cloud environments.
- **Dependency Mapping:** Visualize relationships between CIs for deeper understanding and impact analysis.
- **Integration Capabilities:** ServiceNow easily integrates with monitoring, provisioning, and other IT tools, enriching your CMDB data.

Conclusion

A robust CMDB is your IT crystal ball. It enhances decision-making, streamlines troubleshooting, and minimizes unintended disruptions. Investing time and resources into your CMDB pays huge dividends across your IT operations.

In our next chapter, we'll discuss how to expand upon this foundation and harness the full potential of your CMDB for even greater value.

Additional Resources

- **ServiceNow CMDB Overview**
  https://docs.servicenow.com/bundle/quebec-it-service-management/page/product/configuration-management/concept/c_CMDB.html
- **The Importance of a CMDB**
  https://www.servicenow.com/solutions/configuration-management-database.html

Harnessing CMDB Potential: Advanced Configurations and Integration

In this chapter, we'll discuss advanced configurations, strategic integrations, and how to maximize the value derived from this ITSM powerhouse. Harness the full might of your CMDB to drive better business outcomes and transform IT operations.

Advanced Configuration Techniques

- **Custom CI Classes:** Go beyond the out-of-the-box CI types. If it's important to your organization, create custom CI classes to track specialized items like business processes, key contracts, or external dependencies.
- **Enhancing Attributes:** Standard CMDB attributes are a starting point. Add custom fields to track data relevant to your specific processes – cost center codes, warranty dates, support team assignments, etc.
- **Lifecycle Status:** Track CIs through their lifecycle (e.g., 'Deployed,' 'Retired,' 'In Repair'). This aids in capacity planning, asset management, and compliance.
- **Relationship Refinement:** Define custom relationship types to model how CIs interact. This could include 'communicates with,' 'is backed up by,' 'depends on,' and more.

The CMDB as Your Integration Hub

Maximize the value of your CMDB by connecting it strategically with other IT tools:

- **Monitoring Tools:**
  - **Real-time Status:** Automatically update CI status in the CMDB based on alerts (e.g., server marked 'down' if monitoring detects failure).
  - **Event-Driven Discovery:** New devices detected by monitoring tools can trigger discovery updates within your CMDB.
- **Deployment & Provisioning Tools:**
  - **Automated CMDB Updates:** Provisioning a new virtual machine should trigger automatic creation or updates of its CI record.
  - **Source of Truth:** Use your CMDB as the authoritative reference for what *should* be deployed, aiding configuration drift prevention.

- **Cloud Management Platforms:**
  - ○ **Visibility of Cloud Resources** Import configuration data for cloud services, VMs, storage, etc., enabling a hybrid infrastructure overview.
  - ○ **Cost Tracking:** Link cloud resource CIs with cost data for chargeback or budgeting analysis at the service level.
- **Vulnerability Scanners**
  - ○ **Proactive Risk Management:** Populate your CMDB with discovered vulnerabilities, prioritizing remediation based on criticality.
  - ○ **Software Version Tracking:** Detect outdated software versions across servers, aiding patch management decisions.
- **Security Information & Event Management (SIEM):**
  - ○ **Incident Enrichment:** CMDB data provides context during security incidents – what service is impacted? Who owns the affected CI?
  - ○ **Configuration Anomaly Detection:** Compare CMDB records with SIEM data to detect unauthorized or unexpected changes.

Advanced Use Cases

Let's look at practical applications of a supercharged CMDB:

- **Cost Analysis:**
  - ○ **Service Costing:** Combine financial data associated with CIs (hardware, software, support contracts) to calculate the true cost of delivering IT services.
  - ○ **Optimization:** Identify underutilized or over-provisioned resources, guiding right-sizing or consolidation decisions.
- **Capacity Planning:**
  - ○ **Proactive Approach:** Analyze CMDB data alongside growth trends to predict when servers, storage, or network capacity will be exhausted.
  - ○ **New Service Impact:** Estimate the resource needs of new service offerings before they launch.
- **Business Continuity & Disaster Recovery:**
  - ○ **Criticality Mapping:** Visually identify the most critical CIs that underpin business-critical services, prioritizing recovery efforts.
  - ○ **Recovery Planning:** Document recovery sequences and dependencies within the CMDB, ensuring a structured plan.

ServiceNow for Enhanced CMDB Power

- **Guided CMDB Setup:** Leverage ServiceNow's guided setup experiences to streamline the initial configuration of your CMDB.
- **Discovery Patterns:** Utilize pre-built patterns to speed up the discovery of common devices, applications, and cloud resources.
- **Integration Hub:** Explore a vast library of pre-built integrations with ITSM tools and platforms to seamlessly enrich your CMDB data.

Remember: CMDB is More than a Database

- **Strategic Vision:** Align your CMDB's development with your organization's goals, prioritizing CIs and integrations that support critical decisions.
- **Change Management Integration:** Ensure any changes to CIs are reflected in the CMDB, and conversely, that changes consider CMDB data.
- **Data Quality:** Repeatedly emphasize the importance of clean data to your IT teams. The CMDB is only as good as what you put into it!

Conclusion

By strategically extending your CMDB and harnessing the power of integrations, you transform it into a proactive decision-making engine. Your CMDB is central to improving efficiency, agility, and minimizing risk across your IT operations.

Next, let's discuss how to ensure your CMDB investment remains sustainable through data governance and careful maintenance.

Additional Resources

- **ServiceNow CMDB Best Practices**
  https://docs.servicenow.com/bundle/quebec-it-service-management/page/product/configuration-management/concept/c_CMDBBestPractices.html
- **Integration Strategies for CMDB**
  https://www.atlassian.com/it-service-management/configuration-management

CMDB Optimization: Data Governance and Maintenance

Let's get down to the business of ensuring your CMDB remains accurate, reliable, and supports your IT organization for the long haul. This chapter will focus on data governance and best practices to maintain the value of your CMDB investment. A CMDB is not a 'set it and forget it' endeavor. Just as your IT infrastructure evolves, so must the processes and focus around your CMDB to ensure it remains a trusted source of truth.

Data Governance: Establishing the Framework

- **CMDB Owner:** No CMDB can thrive without a clearly designated champion – an individual or team responsible for its health and strategic direction.
- **Data Owners:** Identify owners for different CI types (e.g., Server team owns server CIs, Applications team owns application CIs). These are your guardians of data quality.
- **Governance Plan:** A living document outlining:
  - Standards for CI creation and updates
  - Processes for access control and permissions
  - Frequency of data audits and reconciliation
  - What constitutes 'core' or mandatory CMDB data
- **Communication is Key:** Governance isn't just about rules. Promote the value of a complete CMDB across IT, and how it benefits everyone's work.

Maintenance Best Practices

1. **Automated Discovery is Your Friend**
   - **Regular Scans:** Configure ServiceNow Discovery and integrations with monitoring tools to run on a schedule, updating your CMDB automatically.
   - **Targeted Discovery:** Don't just scan everything. Focus on what matters within the scope of your CMDB's goals.
   - **Discovery Reconciliation:** Implement processes to reconcile automatically discovered data with manually entered records to prevent conflicts.

2. **Change Management Integration is Crucial**
   - **Two-Way Street:** Change records should reference affected CIs, and ideally, CI records should reflect that they were modified as part of a change.
   - **Automated Updates:** Explore ways to have approved changes push certain CI attribute updates directly into the CMDB to avoid manual errors.
3. **Data Quality Reviews**
   - **Scheduled Audits:** Regularly audit a sample of CI types, examining records for completeness, outdated values, or inaccuracies.
   - **Spot Checks:** Tie CMDB spot checks to your Problem Management process. If an incident points to incorrect data, use that as a learning moment to fix the source.
   - **Data Validation Rules:** Configure your CMDB where possible to enforce data entry standards (e.g., date fields in the correct format, required fields).
4. **CMDB Cleanup**
   - **Lifecycle Driven:** Actively retire or mark CIs as decommissioned when they reach end-of-life. Avoid a cluttered CMDB.
   - **Identify Orphaned CIs:** Periodically identify CIs with no clear relationships. If they don't serve a purpose, they might need removal.
   - **Archiving Strategy:** For historical analysis or audit purposes, develop a strategy for archiving old CMDB data.

Key Considerations

- **User Access & Permissions:** Implement role-based access to control who can modify different areas of your CMDB, particularly for critical CIs.
- **Metrics:** Track metrics related to CMDB health:
  - **Completeness:** Percentage of core CIs that have mandatory fields filled.
  - **Accuracy:** As measured by audits or incidents/problems caused by bad data.
  - **Usage:** Are people actively using the CMDB for troubleshooting, change planning, or decision-making?
- **Data Trust:** Regular communication of data quality improvements and wins fosters trust in the CMDB, encouraging wider adoption.

ServiceNow Features to Simplify Maintenance

- **CMDB Health Dashboard:** Provides customizable, at-a-glance metrics on CMDB completeness, correctness, and compliance.
- **Data Certification:** Schedule certifications where data owners review and attest to the accuracy of CI records under their purview.
- **ServiceNow HealthLog Analytics:** Helps you analyze the potential root causes of CMDB data issues to proactively address the source.

Continuous Improvement for Your CMDB

- **Review Your Governance:** Does your CMDB governance plan evolve with your organization's needs or changes in technology? Review at least annually.
- **Feedback:** Survey users regarding the CMDB's usefulness and pain points. Do they find what they need easily? Are there consistent issues?
- **Tie to Initiatives:** When you expand your CMDB or integrate it with new tools, clearly communicate the 'why' to IT teams to boost buy-in.

Conclusion

A well-maintained CMDB is the bedrock of informed IT decisions. Through defined governance, regular maintenance, and a focus on quality, you'll ensure your CMDB remains a strategic asset rather than a mere data warehouse.

Next up, let's dive into Knowledge Management, another pillar for IT service excellence.

Additional Resources

- **CMDB Data Governance Framework**
  https://docs.servicenow.com/bundle/quebec-it-service-management/page/product/configuration-management/concept/c_CMDBDataGovernance.html
- **Data Certification in ServiceNow**
  https://docs.servicenow.com/bundle/quebec-platform-administration/page/administer/data-management/concept/c_DataCertification.html

Knowledge Management Essentials: Building a Foundation

This chapter lays the groundwork for establishing effective Knowledge Management (KM) practices within ServiceNow. Knowledge Management is about capturing, structuring, and making accessible the solutions, workarounds, and insights that would otherwise live only within the heads of your IT staff.

Why Knowledge Management Matters

- **Resolve Issues Faster:** Frontline teams find answers quickly, reducing MTTR and freeing up experts from repetitive questions.
- **Empower Self-Service:** Well-designed knowledge bases enable users to resolve their own basic issues, reducing ticket volume.
- **Prevent Recurring Problems:** Analyzing knowledge usage patterns can help Problem Management identify areas for deeper fixes.
- **Preserve Expertise:** Ensure knowledge isn't lost due to staff turnover or team reassignments.
- **Onboarding & Training:** A knowledge base accelerates the onboarding process for new IT employees or users transitioning to new systems.

Key Concepts

- **Knowledge-Centered Support (KCS):** A popular KM methodology emphasizing knowledge capture as a byproduct of resolving incidents and requests.
- **Knowledge Lifecycle:** The process of creating, reviewing, approving, publishing, using, and ultimately retiring or archiving knowledge articles.
- **Knowledge Base Structure:** Thoughtful categorization enables users to easily discover relevant knowledge.

Core Building Blocks: Setting the Stage

1. **KM Strategy**
   - **Scope:** What types of knowledge will you focus on? User-facing, internal IT, process documentation? Clearly define your KM goals.
   - **Ownership:** Who is responsible for the overall health of your knowledge base? Establish a KM champion or team.
2. **Technology: ServiceNow as Your Platform**

- ○ **Knowledge Base Creation:** ServiceNow offers easy tools to create knowledge bases with rich text formatting and the ability to attach files.
- ○ **Search:** A robust search engine is crucial, including the ability to find content within attachments.
- ○ **Workflow:** Consider simple approval workflows before articles are published, especially for externally-facing knowledge.

3. **Culture Shift**
   - ○ **Incentivize Knowledge Sharing:** Recognize and reward both the creation and use of good knowledge articles.
   - ○ **Make It a Habit:** Emphasize the importance of documenting solutions as part of every incident and request closure.
   - ○ **Don't Reinvent the Wheel:** Train staff to search the existing knowledge base before escalating or starting time-consuming troubleshooting.

Knowledge Article Best Practices

- **Clear, Concise Titles:** Help users at a glance know if an article is relevant to them.
- **Simple Structure:** Use consistent templates for different types of knowledge (Troubleshooting, How-To, Known Error).
- **Target Audience:** Is this for the service desk, internal IT, or end-users? Tailor the language and technical depth.
- **Ownership & Review:** Assign an owner and set a schedule for periodic review to ensure articles don't become outdated.

Getting Started - Focus is Key

- **Choose a Pilot Project:** Start with a defined area – a well-understood service or a team that's already inclined towards documentation.
- **Metrics:** Define what you'll measure (article creation, views, feedback ratings, reduction in duplicate tickets) to gauge KM success.
- **Iterate:** Gather feedback early and often. Are people finding the knowledge base easy to use and helpful? Don't be afraid to course-correct.

ServiceNow Features to Support Your KM

- **User Permissions:** Control who can create, edit, and publish knowledge within different knowledge bases.

- **Feedback Mechanisms:** Enable users to rate articles or leave comments, providing valuable insights into knowledge quality.
- **Text Analytics:** ServiceNow can analyze unstructured data like incident descriptions to suggest potential article creation.

Conclusion

Building a thriving knowledge base takes time, dedication, and continuous improvement. By starting with a solid foundation, aligning KM with your IT goals, and nurturing a culture of knowledge sharing, you'll transform your IT support model.

In our next chapter, we'll delve into advanced techniques to take your Knowledge Management capabilities to the next level.

Additional Resources

- **ServiceNow Knowledge Management**
  https://docs.servicenow.com/bundle/quebec-servicenow-platform/page/use/knowledge-management/concept/knowledge-management.html
- **Knowledge-Centered Support (KCS) Principles**
  https://docs.servicenow.com/bundle/quebec-it-service-management/page/product/knowledge-management/task/kcs-principles.html
- **Best Practices for Creating a Knowledge Base**
  https://docs.servicenow.com/bundle/quebec-servicenow-platform/page/use/knowledge-management/task/knowledge-best-practices.html

Advanced Knowledge Management Techniques: Implementation Strategies

With a solid KM foundation established, it's time to focus on techniques that promote continuous improvement, user engagement, and deeper integration with your IT processes.

Strategy 1: Knowledge in the Flow of Work

- **Contextual Knowledge:** Surface relevant knowledge articles directly within incident, problem, and request forms where technicians work.
- **Case Swarming:** Utilize collaboration tools within ServiceNow for frontline teams to solve issues together, documenting solutions as they go. Promote real-time KM.
- **AI-Powered Suggestions:** Explore ServiceNow's AI Search capabilities to proactively suggest knowledge articles based on ticket short descriptions.

Strategy 2: Gamification & Incentivization

- **Reward Contribution:** Implement a point system where users earn recognition or tangible rewards for creating high-quality, well-used articles.
- **Healthy Competition:** Leaderboards can visualize top knowledge contributors within teams or across the organization (use with sensitivity).
- **Celebrate KM Wins:** Regularly highlight success stories where proper KM use significantly reduced resolution time or prevented escalations.

Strategy 3: Focusing on Findability

- **Leverage Search Analytics:** Monitor what users are searching for and identify gaps. Are there common terms without results? Is your KM content missing?
- **SEO for Your Knowledge Base:** Think like your users. Use keywords they would naturally use and consider synonyms in your article titles and content.
- **Continuously Refine Structure:** As your knowledge base grows, regularly review your categorization scheme to ensure it remains intuitive.

Strategy 4: Knowledge as a Proactive Tool

- **Self-Service Deflection:** Design your knowledge portal with deflection in mind. Analyze top call drivers and create prominent, easy-to-follow solutions.
- **Automated Notifications:** Utilize workflows to proactively send users relevant articles when new known errors are published, or there's an outage affecting their service.
- **Targeted Training:** If knowledge articles are frequently linked to incidents of a specific nature, create targeted training for the responsible team.

Strategy 5: Harnessing User Feedback

- **Simple Feedback Mechanisms:** 'Was this helpful?' thumbs up/down ratings on articles provide rapid insight without overwhelming users.
- **In-Depth Surveys:** Periodically send users surveys focusing on the ease of finding information, and if the knowledge base helps them do their jobs better.
- **User Communities:** If feasible, foster a knowledge forum where users help each other, surfacing frequently requested content to the KM team.

Strategy 6: Linking Knowledge to Your CMDB

- **Problem Management Insights:** Identify CIs commonly involved in incidents or problems. Attach relevant troubleshooting articles directly to CI records.
- **Change Preparation:** During change planning, link knowledge articles about the affected CIs to the change record for easy reference by implementation teams.
- **Vulnerability Alerts:** Link articles detailing remediation steps to affected CIs when vulnerabilities are discovered, streamlining the action plan.

ServiceNow Tools to Optimize KM

- **Performance Analytics for KM:** Track article views, creation rates, search trends, feedback, and link metrics to incident deflection or reduced MTTR.
- **Contextual Search:** Embed a search bar within forms for technicians to find relevant articles without leaving their workspace.

- **Virtual Agent for Knowledge:** Build Virtual Agent topics that guide users towards self-service solutions and escalate to live agent support only if needed.

Remember:

- **KM Champions:** Identify KM advocates within different teams to promote adoption and contribute to your knowledge base.
- **Metrics That Matter:** Focus on metrics tied to real IT improvements – not just quantity of articles.
- **Iterative Approach:** Regularly assess the effectiveness of your KM strategies and be prepared to adjust course based on data and feedback.

Conclusion

Advanced Knowledge Management transforms knowledge into a strategic asset that empowers both your IT teams and end-users. By focusing on usability, incentivization, and integration with other ITSM processes, you'll create a knowledge-centric service culture that benefits everyone.

In our next chapter, we'll discuss ensuring your knowledge base stays valuable and effective through proper curation and lifecycle management.

Additional Resources

- **Gamification in Knowledge Management**
  https://docs.servicenow.com/bundle/quebec-it-service-management/page/product/knowledge-management/concept/gamification.html
- **AI and Knowledge Management**
  https://www.techtarget.com/searchenterpriseai/

Knowledge Management Optimization: Content Curation and Accessibility

Let's get into the nitty-gritty of ensuring your knowledge base remains a reliable, well-maintained source of information. This chapter focuses on content curation to maximize value and accessibility considerations to serve diverse user needs. Even a well-designed knowledge base can become cluttered over time. Knowledge, just like your IT environment, needs lifecycle management to remain helpful and not become a hurdle.

Strategy 1: Knowledge Content Curation

- **Appoint Content Curators:** Assign ownership of specific knowledge domains to subject matter experts. They are your knowledge quality control.
- **Regular Spring Cleaning:** Establish a schedule for reviewing articles. Start with the most used, and those linked to the most incidents.
- **Archiving vs. Deletion:** Preserve old versions for historical reference if needed, but remove outdated articles from frontline search results.
- **Sunset Policy:** Clearly mark articles about to be retired, allowing time for relevant content to be migrated to an updated version, if necessary.
- **Knowledge Base Health Analytics:** Track the average age of articles, identify unused articles, and get an overall picture of your content landscape.

Strategy 2: Accessibility for Everyone

- **Diverse User Needs:** Your users have different roles, technical levels, and preferences. Consider how best to cater to those variances.
- **Multiple Knowledge Bases:** For large organizations, sometimes it makes sense to segment knowledge into a more advanced internal IT knowledge base and a simplified outward-facing knowledge base for end-users.
- **Plain Language:** Avoid unnecessary jargon and overly technical explanations, especially for user-facing content.
- **Visuals & Multimedia:** Supplement text with screenshots, process flow diagrams, or even short video tutorials to cater to different learning styles.
- **ADA Compliance:** Make sure your knowledge base adheres to accessibility guidelines (screen reader friendly, alternative text for images, etc.)

Strategy 3: Leveraging Knowledge Analytics

- **Search Analytics Are Your Friend:** Identify what users frequently search for but don't find results. These gaps highlight content opportunities.
- **Article Feedback Insights:** Analyze negative ratings and user comments. Are they struggling with outdated info or unclear explanations?
- **Linking Analytics:** Understand which articles are heavily used in conjunction with specific incident or problem types.

Strategy 4: Driving Knowledge Reuse

- **Make Reuse Rewarding:** If KM incentives exist, include metrics related to utilizing existing knowledge to solve incidents and requests faster.
- **Spotlighting Success:** When an existing knowledge article proves exceptionally useful, highlight it – showing how it saved time or prevented a future problem.
- **Template Integration:** Embed knowledge article search or links to relevant articles within standard troubleshooting templates, prompting reuse.

Strategy 5: Accessibility on Multiple Channels

- **Knowledge on the Service Portal:** Integrate a knowledge search bar prominently on your service portal for ease of self-service by end-users.
- **Mobile Access:** Ensure your knowledge base is responsive or accessible via a mobile app for technicians needing solutions in the field.
- **Chatbots & Virtual Agents:** Train your ServiceNow Virtual Agent to search the knowledge base and offer article snippets directly within conversations.

ServiceNow Tools to Amplify Your Efforts

- **Article Versioning:** Track changes and maintain a history of past versions of knowledge articles.
- **Translation Functionality:** Enable multilingual support for knowledge bases serving global users.
- **Accessibility Checker:** Built-in tools to assess your knowledge articles for ADA compliance.

- **Feedback Loop Integration:** Link user feedback on articles directly to incident or problem records for deeper visibility.

Remember:

- **Don't Neglect Formatting:** Well-structured articles with headings, clear formatting, and visuals improve readability, which impacts user comprehension.
- **Metadata Matters:** Use appropriate tags and keywords to enhance search results and discoverability.
- **Accessibility as Inclusion:** Make accessibility a core part of your KM design, not an afterthought, to create an inclusive knowledge-sharing environment.

Conclusion

Optimized knowledge management requires a continuous focus on content quality, accessibility, and alignment with evolving user needs. By actively managing your knowledge lifecycle and prioritizing user experience, you create a knowledge base that truly empowers your organization.

Up next, let's explore the world of Service Level Management and learn how to set, track, and achieve the IT service quality your users expect!

Additional Resources

- **Web Content Accessibility Guidelines (WCAG)**
  https://www.w3.org/WAI/standards-guidelines/wcag/
- **Tips for Making a Knowledge Base Accessible**
  https://docs.servicenow.com/bundle/quebec-servicenow-platform/page/use/knowledge-management/task/making-knowledge-accessible.html

Mastering Service Level Management: Key Principles and Practices

Service Level Management is the bridge between IT and its customers – ensuring a shared understanding of what services are delivered, at what levels, and how success will be measured.

Why Service Level Management Matters

- **Sets Clear Expectations:** SLM prevents mismatched expectations by clearly defining what users can expect from IT in terms of availability, performance, and support responsiveness
- **Customer Satisfaction:** By meeting or exceeding agreed-upon service levels, IT builds trust and fosters a positive relationship with its users.
- **Drives Process Improvement:** Tracking performance against SLAs highlights areas where IT processes might be a bottleneck, leading to targeted refinements .
- **Demonstrates IT Value:** SLM reporting provides tangible evidence of IT's contribution to business goals.
- **Cost Accountability:** SLAs can help align IT spending with the true cost of delivering a specific level of service.

Key Concepts

- **Service Level Agreement (SLA):** A formal contract between the IT service provider and the customer (internal department or external). It outlines service deliverables, metrics, and consequences for not meeting targets.
- **Operational Level Agreement (OLA):** Agreements between internal IT teams underpinning SLAs. For example, the infrastructure team might have an OLA with the application team regarding database uptime to support a customer-facing SLA.
- **Underpinning Contracts (UC):** Agreements with external vendors or suppliers that support IT's ability to deliver on its SLAs.

Core SLM Process Activities

1. **Identify Critical Services:** Not everything needs an SLA. Focus on services that directly impact business operations or have a high volume of users.

2. **Metrics That Matter:** Define measurable metrics tied to user experience (e.g., availability percentage, incident resolution time, average page load speed).
3. **Negotiate Realistic Targets:** SLAs should be achievable, but also push for better performance. Find a balance between ambition and practicality.
4. **Reporting & Reviews:** Regularly review performance against SLAs. Discuss underperformance, root causes, and improvement plans transparently.
5. **Continuous Improvement:** SLM is not static. As business needs and technology change, so should your SLAs and the underlying IT processes supporting them.

Building Effective SLAs

- **Clear and Unambiguous:** Avoid jargon and complex language. SLAs should be understandable to both IT staff and non-technical stakeholders.
- **Balance Specificity and Flexibility:** Be specific about metrics and targets, but allow some room for unforeseen circumstances (e.g., exclusions during planned maintenance).
- **Escalation Procedures:** Outline what happens when SLAs are breached. Include a tiered approach with clear communication paths.
- **Tied to Consequences:** Consider meaningful impact (e.g., service credits, management attention) for consistent underperformance. But don't make it just punitive.

ServiceNow for SLM Success

- **SLA Workflows:** Define the steps involved in negotiating, activating, monitoring, and reporting on SLAs.
- **SLA Definition:** ServiceNow allows you to configure SLA conditions based on various triggers in incident, problem, or change records.
- **Dashboards & Reporting:** Visualize SLA performance in real-time, drill into historical data, and quickly identify services at risk of SLA breaches.
- **OLA and UC Management:** Track OLAs and underpinning contracts alongside SLAs for a complete picture of service level dependencies.

Important Considerations

- **Start Simple, Then Expand:** Begin with a few key services, master the SLM process, and then gradually add more.

- **Communication is Key:** Actively communicate SLA performance and changes to stakeholders. Transparency builds trust.
- **Don't Overpromise:** SLM failure often lies in setting unattainable targets. Honesty and realism are critical.

Conclusion

Effective Service Level Management establishes IT as a reliable partner, not just a reactive fix-it shop. By proactively managing service quality and driving continuous improvement, you'll transform how IT is perceived within your organization.

In our next chapter, we'll delve into the specifics of creating SLAs, best practices, and common pitfalls to avoid.

Additional Resources

- **ServiceNow Service Level Management**
  https://docs.servicenow.com/bundle/quebec-it-service-management/page/product/service-level-management/concept/c_ServiceLevelManagement.html

Service Level Agreements (SLAs) Demystified: Implementation Guidelines

In the previous chapter, we discussed the principles behind Service Level Management. Now, we focus on SLAs – the tangible embodiment of these principles. Think of SLAs as the rulebook that guides the IT-customer relationship.

Key Considerations Before You Start

- **SLM Framework First:** Ensure you have a basic Service Level Management process in place. SLAs are meaningless without a process for tracking, reporting, and acting upon them.
- **Executive Support:** Successful SLAs require buy-in from both IT leadership and the business stakeholders they serve.
- **Mutual Agreement:** SLAs should never be a tool IT imposes upon its customers, but rather a collaboratively defined contract.

Step-by-Step Guide to SLA Creation

1. **Identify the 'Why' Behind the SLA**
   - What is the service this SLA will cover? Is it to reduce downtime, provide faster onboarding, or something else entirely?
   - What business value or outcome does this SLA seek to protect?
2. **Choose Meaningful Metrics**
   - **Avoid Vanity Metrics:** Don't just measure what's easy. Ensure metrics align with a true user experience improvement.
   - **Common SLA Metrics:**
     - Availability (Uptime %)
     - Incident Resolution Time (based on priority)
     - Request Fulfillment Time
     - Customer Satisfaction (CSAT scores)
   - **Consider a Tiered Approach:** Different customer groups might have different needs. Basic support vs. 'always-on' premium support could have varied SLA targets.
3. **Set Baseline Performance**
   - Honest Analysis Matters:** Use historical data to understand current service levels honestly, before inflating targets.
   - Start Achievable:** Encourage further improvement, but don't set yourself up for immediate failure with impossible targets.
4. **Defining the Fine Print**

- Measurement Periods: When does the SLA clock start and stop? 24x7? Business hours? Be explicit.
- Exclusions: Planned maintenance, outages outside IT's control (e.g., power company issues) should be pre-defined.
- Change Management Interaction: How do planned changes impact SLA calculations? Define this clearly to avoid conflict.

5. Consequences & Escalations
   - Impact Over Punishment: Focus on what actions will be taken if SLAs are missed (e.g., prioritized problem investigation, higher management focus).
   - Meaningful But Not Crippling: Service credits (refunds) can be a tool, but if excessive, make delivering the service itself unsustainable.
   - Escalation Path: Who gets notified, at what tiers of underperformance, and when.

6. The Operational Details
   - Incident/Request Prioritization: Ensure your incident and request management processes have the fields and workflows to align with SLA-based prioritization.
   - Regular Reporting: How often will SLA reports be generated and shared with stakeholders? (Monthly, quarterly).

7. Formal Review & Approval
   - All Parties Involved: This includes IT, customer representatives, and potentially legal or procurement teams depending on your organization.

ServiceNow for SLA Success

- **SLA Task Creation:** Break down SLA conditions within workflows (e.g., a different task gets created if an incident breaches its resolution target).
- **SLA Attachments:** Attach the SLA document itself to relevant incident, change, or problem records for clarity.
- **Real-time SLA Clocks:** Visual displays on dashboards showing time remaining or potential breaches help IT teams stay proactive.

Common SLA Pitfalls & How to Avoid Them

- **SLA Proliferation:** Too many SLAs become impossible to manage. Focus on those truly critical to the business.
- **Metrics Misinterpretation:** Ensure all stakeholders understand what the metric truly measures and how it's calculated.

- **Set and Forget:** SLAs should evolve. Set a regular review cadence (annually or bi-annually) to adjust as needs change.

Conclusion

Well-designed SLAs create a shared understanding of expectations and drive a focus on delivering a consistent quality of service. By carefully considering the elements discussed, you'll transform SLAs from a source of friction to a tool for collaboration and continuous improvement.

In our next chapter, we'll discuss how to optimize SLM through performance metrics and reporting best practices.

Additional Resources

- **SLA Best Practices**
  https://docs.servicenow.com/bundle/quebec-it-service-management/page/product/service-level-management/task/t_SLABestPractices.html
- **Common SLA Mistakes**
  https://docs.servicenow.com/bundle/quebec-it-service-management/page/product/service-level-management/task/t_CommonSLAMistakes.html

Service Level Management Optimization: Metrics and Performance Improvement

Let's get down to the business of taking your Service Level Management from good to great. In this chapter, we'll focus on metrics-driven decision-making and how to turn SLM data into actionable improvements. Remember, SLAs are not just about hitting targets – they're about using the data they generate to drive a cycle of continuous IT service improvement.

Beyond the Basics: Metrics That Matter

- **Focus on Trends:** Individual breaches matter, but spotting patterns over time is more valuable for systemic change (e.g., recurring issues at a specific time of day).
- **Customer Sentiment:** Customer Satisfaction Scores (CSAT) tied to incidents or service requests add a qualitative layer to your quantifiable metrics.
- **Problem & Change Correlation:** Track if problems you fix have a tangible positive impact on SLA compliance. Do changes inadvertently cause SLA drops?
- **Cost per Metric:** For select SLAs, track the cost of resources (staff time, tools) in providing the agreed-upon service level. This aids in value justification.

Key Performance Indicators (KPIs) for SLM

KPIs are high-level aggregations of your SLA data that provide insights into overall SLM health. Examples include:

- **Overall SLA Compliance Percentage:** Across all your active SLAs, what percentage are meeting their targets on a rolling basis (e.g., over the past month)?
- **Average Time to Breach:** When SLAs are missed, how quickly does it happen? This can signal lack of prioritization or insufficient resources.
- **SLA Improvement Over Time:** Are you seeing a consistent upward trend in compliance as processes mature?
- **SLAs Tied to Business Outcomes:** Can you correlate better SLA performance with things like increased sales, customer retention, or employee productivity?

The Power of Reporting & Dashboards

1. **Target Your Audience**
   - **IT Teams:** Need operational level dashboards focused on at-risk SLAs, with immediate drill-down to problem areas.
   - **Stakeholders:** Non-technical reports focused on overall trends, significant improvements achieved, and future plans.
   - **Executives:** High-level KPIs demonstrating SLM's impact and justifying investment in IT services.
2. **Visualizations that Tell a Story**
   - **Simple is Powerful:** Line charts showing SLA performance against targets over time tell the story of improvement at a glance.
   - **Comparisons:** Compare performance across similar services, time periods, or customer groups to uncover underperforming areas.
   - **Problem & Change Impacts:** Overlay problem spikes and changes on SLA performance charts to visualize their impact
3. **Actionable, Not Just Informative**
   - **Automated Alerts:** Configure notifications for SLAs about to breach, not just when they've already failed.
   - **Problem Management Trigger** Recurring SLA misses related to a specific CI or service should trigger problem investigations proactively.

Using SLM Data to Drive Improvements

- **Target Root Causes, Not Symptoms:** Simple breach fixes like extending SLA targets might seem appealing but don't solve underlying problems.
- **Process Bottlenecks:** Do resolution times suggest your incident management process has steps that cause unnecessary delays?
- **Training Needs:** Consistently missed SLAs in a specific area might indicate a team needs targeted training or updated knowledge articles.
- **Capacity Planning:** Are SLAs consistently missed during peak times? Investigate capacity and staffing needs.
- **Self-Service Success:** Analyze SLA compliance for incidents submitted through self-service. Are you effectively deflecting simple issues?

ServiceNow for SLM Optimization

- **Performance Analytics:** Dig deep with historical trends, pre-built KPI visualizations, and the ability to create your own custom dashboards.
- **Reporting:** Create scheduled reports, exportable in various formats for different audiences.
- **Integration Potential:** Explore pulling in data from monitoring, capacity management, or project management tools to enrich your SLM insights.

Additional Considerations

- **Incentivize the Right Things:** If your IT staff are rewarded solely based on hitting SLA metrics, be aware of unintended consequences (like rushing solutions and causing more problems).
- **Feedback Loops Matter:** Survey customers about the importance of different SLAs. Do they align with the user's true experience?
- **External Benchmarks:** While a useful reference, don't obsess over industry averages. Focus on improving upon your own past performance.

Conclusion

By evolving your SLM practices with a focus on data, you shift IT's focus from purely reactive to proactive service quality management. SLMs become a tool to demonstrate IT's value and position your IT organization as a strategic business partner.

Let me know if you'd like to explore specific SLM reporting best practices or advanced SLA analytics!

Additional Resources

- **How to Use SLM Data for Improvement**
  https://docs.servicenow.com/bundle/quebec-it-service-management/page/product/service-level-management/task/t_UseSLMDataForImprovement.html
- **KPI Examples for IT Service Management**
  https://docs.servicenow.com/bundle/quebec-it-service-management/page/product/service-management-dashboard/concept/kpi-examples-itsm.html

Conclusion

Throughout this book, we've embarked on a journey through the core tenets of IT Service Management and explored how ServiceNow provides a powerful platform to translate those principles into tangible results. Let's recap the key takeaways and look toward the exciting future of IT service delivery.

The Transformative Power of ITSM

ITSM is not another set of rigid rules to follow. It's a fundamental shift in how IT operates. By focusing on delivering value to users, IT transforms from a cost center into a strategic driver of business success. Principles like structured incident and problem management, proactive change implementation, a robust knowledge base, and well-defined service levels elevate the entire IT organization.

ServiceNow: Your ITSM Accelerator

ServiceNow goes beyond being a mere software tool. It's a flexible platform that can scale and adapt alongside your IT maturity. As your understanding of ITSM deepens, ServiceNow provides the framework, workflows, and automation capabilities to continually streamline processes and improve the user experience.

Key Lessons to Remember

- **ITSM is a Journey, Not a Destination:** Continuous improvement is at the heart of this discipline. Analyze metrics, gather feedback, and refine your approach. What works now may need an update in the future due to business changes or technology advancements.
- **The Power of Process:** Documented, well-understood processes empower IT staff, ensuring consistency and efficiency across your teams.
- **Data is Your Guide:** Make decisions driven by metrics generated from within ServiceNow, but don't forget the qualitative side – user satisfaction matters just as much!
- **The CMDB as Your Anchor:** A well-maintained, accurate CMDB is the foundation for informed decision-making at every level of IT.
- **Knowledge is Power:** A knowledge-sharing culture accelerates problem-solving, empowers self-service, and allows your IT team to focus on what they do best.

- **SLAs Build Trust:** Service Level Agreements foster a partnership between IT and its customers based on clarity and shared expectations.

The Future of ITSM: What's Next?

IT Service Management will continue to evolve alongside technology trends. Here's where your focus should be in the coming years:

- **Automation & AI:** Embrace the potential of automation and AI to handle routine tasks, freeing skilled staff to tackle more strategic work and complex problems.
- **The Democratization of IT:** Self-service portals, robust knowledge bases, and chatbots will put solutions directly in the hands of users, reducing strain on IT support teams.
- **Integration as the Norm:** IT services rarely exist in isolation. The ability to integrate ServiceNow seamlessly with the wider IT landscape will become even more critical.
- **IT as Value Driver:** The focus on demonstrating the business impact of IT initiatives through metrics and reporting will only intensify.

Call to Action

You now possess the knowledge and understanding to elevate your IT service delivery with ServiceNow. Implement the strategies from this book, commit to best practices, and champion a culture focused on user experience. Empower yourself to shape IT's role as a driving force for innovation and excellence within your organization.

Thank you for reading, and best of luck on your ITSM journey!

Further Exploration

If you're hungry for more, consider exploring these areas:

- **ITIL Certifications:** Further deepen your ITSM knowledge with formal ITIL training and certifications.
- **ServiceNow Training & Resources:** Expand your technical knowledge with ServiceNow's extensive training options and community forums.
- **Industry Blogs & Webinars** Stay up-to-date on ServiceNow innovation and ITSM best practices through industry publications and webinars.